The Korean Go Associati

LEARN TO PLAY GO
VOLUME III: THE DRAGON STYLE

Janice Kim 1 dan
Jeong Soo-hyun 8 dan

Drawings by **a lee**

Good Move Press

Published by
Good Move Press
105 Duane Street #39D
New York, NY 10007

ISBN 0-9644796-3-X

Printed in U.S.A.

CONTENTS
VOLUME III: THE DRAGON STYLE

Preface

The other day I was looking through a book called *Knock 'em Down and Take 'em Out: Knife Fighting Techniques From Folsom Prison,* in which the author rails against so-called martial arts experts, saying that martial arts training is a lot of stylized nonsense. Ignoring the obvious question—namely, if it's so useless why is the author in prison while the martial artists are appearing in feature films?—I'd like to address what one might call the "foo-foo" factor.

The classic example of the foo-foo factor is the long-term student of karate who knows lots of forms, attends his weekly classes diligently, finally passes the test to become black belt, and then gets beaten up on the way home by the neighborhood bully. As go is also a martial art, the analogue would be the beginning player who studies very hard and has learned a lot of theory, but who's regularly crushed by a player who does everything wrong. When this happens one might indeed question the usefulness of martial arts when knocking 'em down and taking 'em out seems so much more effective.

I think this is a case of the head of the snake meeting the tail of the dragon. The snake may get in a bite or two, but if the dragon gets annoyed it can crush the snake with a sweep of its tail, hardly even tapping its power. But you don't see dragons very often (even though it's up to us which one we want to be).

Acknowledgements

Many thanks to the Good Move Press crew, especially Michael J. Simon, who made this book possible; Angie Lee, who's done my favorite drawings yet; friends and family whose support never flags; and all the reviewers and readers of the *Learn to Play Go* series, especially Barbara London, who gave invaluable help and encouragement. A special thanks to the China Weiqi Association for their help with this volume; to Ahn Sangsoo, provider of dragons; to Brian D'Amato, the Reality Checkpoint Guy; David A. Mechner; and our little brother John Lee. Of course, I manage any errors all by myself.

Janice Kim
June 1, 1996

Preface to the Second Edition

As in the second edition of Volume I, there are a number of changes in this edition of Volume III, including my adoption of the convention of referring to Black as male and White as female, and using some very common go terms such as *hane,* in order to ease a tortured sentence or two. More substantively I've tried to correct some of my errors and omissions, as well as clarify and expand difficult sections, particularly in the nine-stone handicap chapter – a special thanks to None Redmond for her careful and insightful comments on that game.

Volume III is designed to be comprehensible for those who have reached the 15-12 kyu level by various means, or by those who have read the first two volumes. However, I should mention that when reviewing games played by higher kyu or even dan level players, I use much the same commentary as that found in this volume. It's my hope that this book will be beneficial to a wide range of players, and perhaps spark the interest of those non-players who must still be out there.

A note about rank changes – my teacher Mr. Jeong has since the first edition of this book been promoted to the top rank of 9 dan. I remain uncertain as to whether or not I should change his rank, or for that matter the order of his name on the cover (Koreans put their family name first). In the end I decided to keep it the same for now.

A special thanks to design god Michael Samuel for his invaluable work on this edition, and to the indefatigable Bruce Price.

Janice Kim
September 1, 1998

PART ONE
THE DRAGON STYLE

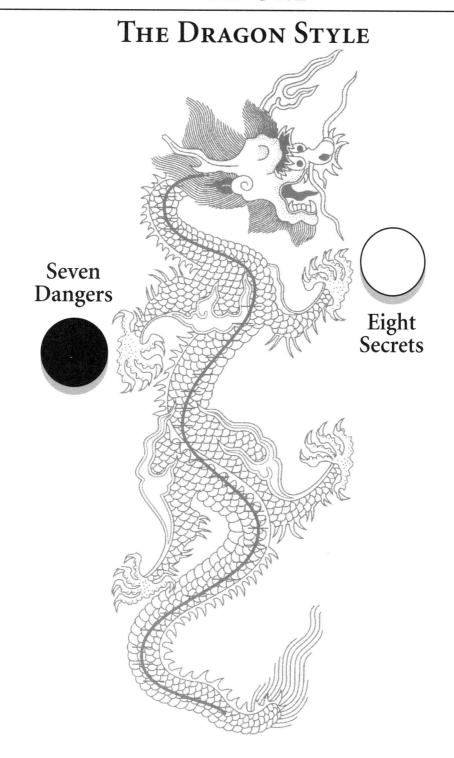

Seven
Dangers

Eight
Secrets

SEVEN DANGERS

« Don't be afraid when you play with a stronger player. Fear is White's strongest ally.»

1. FEAR

Diagram 1.

Here's a classic example of scaring Black in a nine-stone handicap game. White plays at 3 and 5. At this point, many people are afraid the black stone on the right side is in trouble.

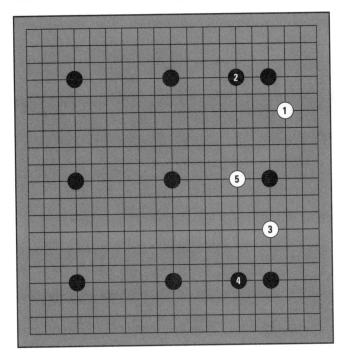

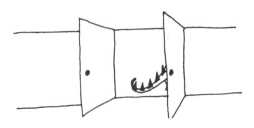

Diagram 2.
So they play Black 6, trying to make **life***
inside. Black continues by playing 8, 10,
12, and 14 to make a **base.** This is a lot
like running and hiding from a flop-
eared rabbit.

Diagram 3.
White 1 intends to frighten Black by
appearing to surround the side **star point**
stone, but White's "surrounding" stones are
actually very weak. There are a lot of help-
ing stones in the area, so Black doesn't
need to be afraid of White 5. The **shoulder
hit** of 6, continuing the pressure up to 10,
is an effective counterattack.

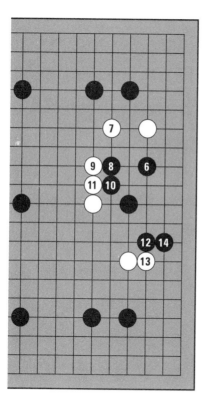

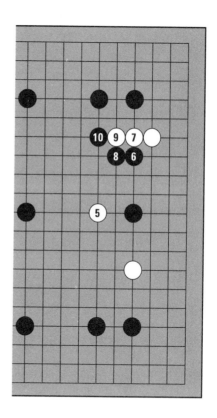

*Terms in **boldface** can be found in the glossary at the end of this book.

❝ *In go, as in any martial art, your mental state is one of the most important factors in winning or losing. You can't play well if you are nervous. Try to relax and stay calm.* **❞**

1. AGITATION

Diagram 4.

Even very strong players make silly mistakes when they are agitated. For example, take a look at this diagram. White played 1. If Black plays at 2, what will happen?

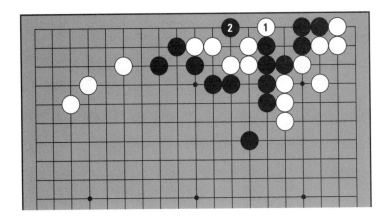

Diagram 5.

White can capture three black stones in a **snapback** with 3. Black ⬠ is a huge blunder. This is the type of simple mistake that actually happens in go.

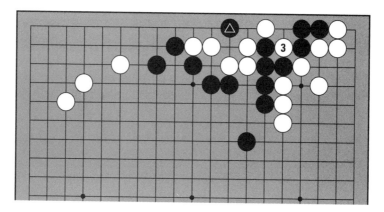

Diagram 6.

Black should calmly consider what White is threatening to do with 1 and protect against the threat by connecting at 2. (Notice if White next plays at A, Black can play at B, and if White B, Black A, so White's group can't make two **eyes.**) Simple mistakes can be avoided if you can think calmly in the heat of battle. You might find that your game improves more from trying to stay calm than from learning any specific moves.

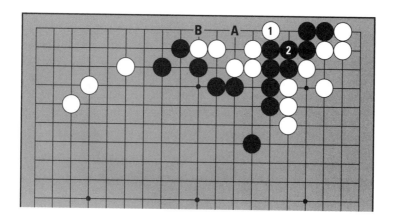

" A greedy play often meets with failure. "

3. GREED

Diagram 7.
Black **pushes** at 1. Even though this group can live now, some people try to **kill** Black by blocking at 2. This is a greedy move.

Diagram 8.
White has a lot of **weak points,** so Black cuts at 3. When White **extends** at 4, Black can play **atari** at 5, and then **double atari** on the marked stones with 7.

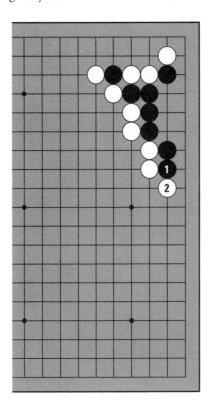

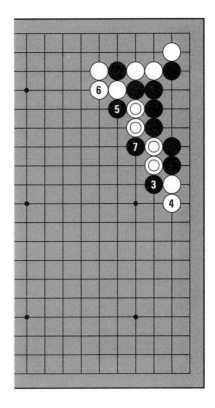

Diagram 9.

In double atari, something has to go. If White escapes at 8, Black captures two stones with 9.

Diagram 10.

This is the result after Black captures. White is separated, and the marked stones are now useless. With the immensely strong **turtle back** exploding into the center, Black has an enormous advantage. White's greedy play has resulted in disaster.

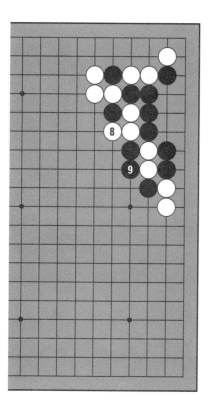

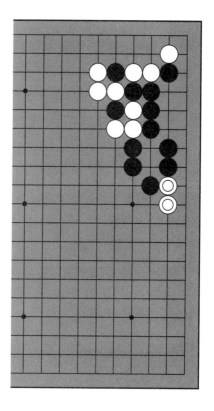

Diagram 11.

Returning to the original position, when Black pushes at 1, there's no need to block. It's enough for White to extend at 2. When Black pushes at 3, White can extend again at 4. White made **thickness** in the center, while Black crawled on the **second line**, so White is very satisfied with this result.

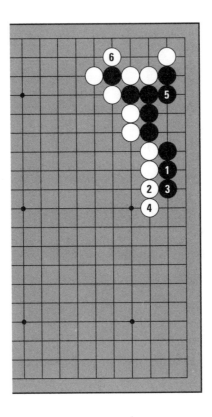

" It's important to think before before every move. Playing automatically is one of the biggest causes of failure. "

4. THOUGHTLESSNESS

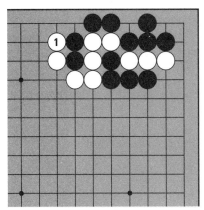

Diagram 12

Diagram 12.
White 1 puts two black stones in atari. If Black connects, what will happen?

Diagram 13.
If Black connects at 2, White plays atari again at 3.

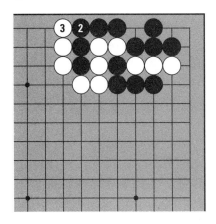

Diagram 14. Black connects at 4 without thinking. Now White can play atari at 5, and Black's ten stones will all be captured.

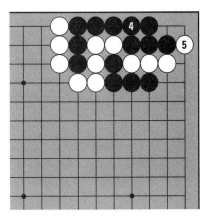

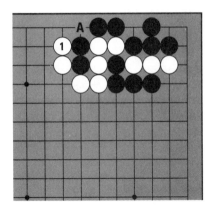

Diagram 15.
When White plays atari at 1, Black has to **read** what will happen after connecting at A. Perhaps more than anything else, reading is the measure of ability in go.

Diagram 16. One big difficulty in reading is that you have to anticipate not just your own moves, but your opponent's. One way to do this is to put yourself in your opponent's shoes and ask, "Why did I play there?" Here's an example. Suppose White **peeps** at 1. What should Black be thinking? He should be considering why White made this move.

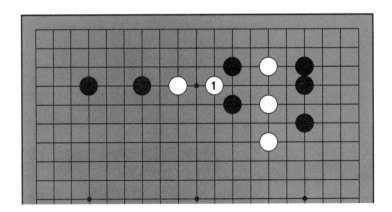

Diagram 17.

The meaning of White ◎: if Black doesn't connect, White plans to push in and cut Black's **one-point jump.** Black's marked stone is cut off without eyes, so a chunk of the upper side falls under White's control.

2 elsewhere

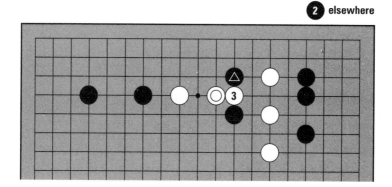

Diagram 18. When White peeps at 1, Black should connect at 2. Now White's two groups are separated and neither has a base, so Black has the advantage in future fighting.

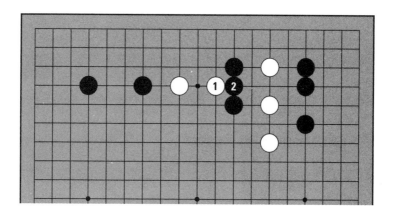

" *Aiming for a result that requires you to play more than one move at a time is nuts, but a common fatal error in go logic. For example, many people play hopeless moves to try to kill stones that can't be killed, or struggle for life after death.* "

5. IRRATIONALITY

Diagram 19.

Black 1 cuts inside White's area, trying to capture White's three stones. This is an unreasonable plan.

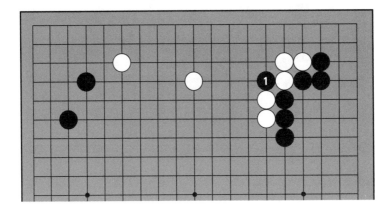

Diagram 20.

Black's plan is to block at 3 and catch three stones. If this could happen, of course it would be good for Black, but expecting this is unreasonable. Your opponent is presumably no fool, and will respond to Black ▲.

② elsewhere

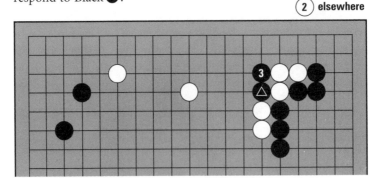

Diagram 21. White can capture the cutting stone in a **ladder.**
Black has failed.

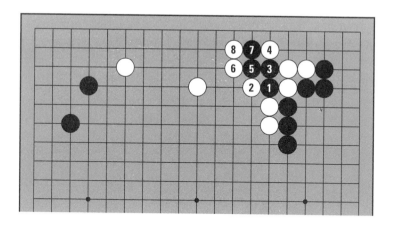

Nei Wei-ping 9 dan (right), widely regarded as the top Chinese player, in a match against
Yoda Norimoto 9 dan of Japan.

❝ There is a Korean expression: Even monkeys fall from trees. Everybody makes mistakes. When you make a mistake, you need to get over it and move on.❞

6. ANGER

Diagram 22.

Black traps a white stone in a ladder at 1. Next, when White plays 2, Black answers at 3. This is a mistake.

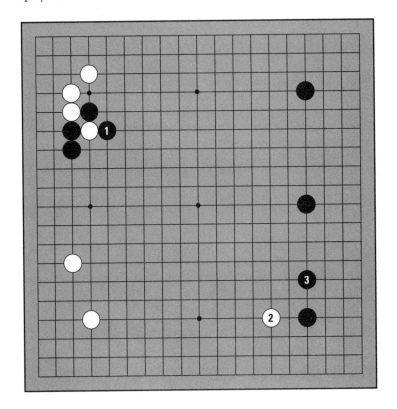

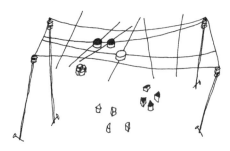

Diagram 23.

Now White can escape at 4. At this point you may get that sinking feeling that there's something you've overlooked: apparently, White ◎ is a **ladder breaker.**

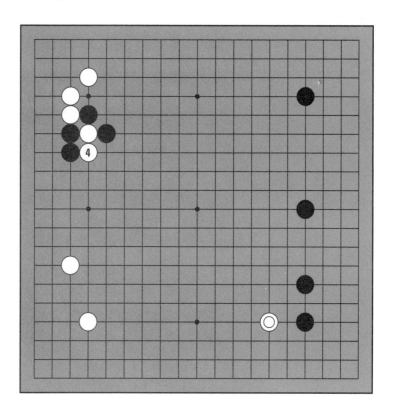

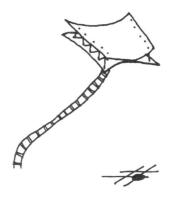

Diagram 24.
Even though the ladder doesn't work, imagine that Black neurotically persists up to 39. White connects to the ladder breaker at 40, and Black has no next move. Many weak points have been created. Since Black can't capture, next White can play double atari all along the sides of the ladder. Black has collapsed because of a psychological inability to recover from one mistake.

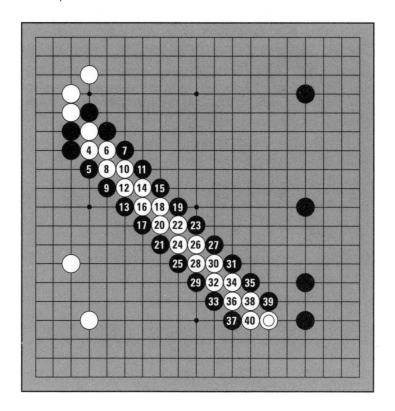

Diagram 25.

When White runs at 4, Black needs to acknowledge the mistake, but not get upset. The ladder doesn't work, so Black extends at 5 to strengthen the two black stones. If White cuts off a stone with 6, Black plays a **two-point jump** to make a base with 7. Even though the marked stone is trapped and Black has suffered a loss, this isn't a decisive mistake. If White plays on the **side star region** at 8, Black can take another side star region at 9, maintaining a kind of balance.

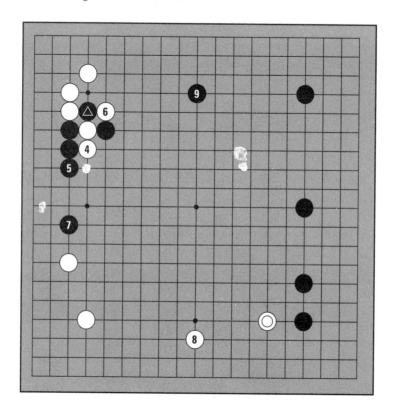

7.   ENVY

" *Everybody wants to win, but thinking too much about winning has a negative effect. You can make many foolish mistakes and overlook some obvious good moves if you are obsessed with winning. Better than thinking about winning is to think about playing well. You can play good go, get stronger, and win more easily this way.*

Try to be a gracious winner and graceful loser. Everybody wins some and loses some, so being too happy about winning or unhappy about losing is shortsighted, as is envy: you don't know who's got the best deal until the very end of the show. "

EIGHT SECRETS

❝ *Go is about making more territory than your opponent. However, many people forget that goal when the opportunity to take prisoners presents itself. It's important not to try to just capture stones, but try to make territory.* **❞**

1. CHOOSE PROFIT OVER GLORY

Diagram 1.

It's White's turn to play. Is it better to catch three black stones at A or to play the **two-point extension** at B?

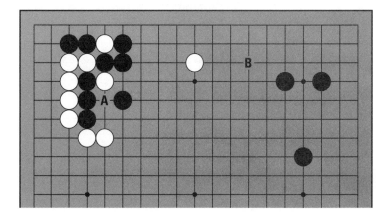

Diagram 2.

It may be tempting to capture with 1 and 3, but then Black gets the huge move at 4. Black 4 enlarges the corner area while attacking White's lone stone.

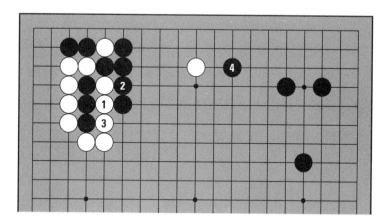

Diagram 3.

White 1 here is better. This move is big for three reasons: it makes a base for White's stone, prevents Black from enlarging the corner area, and gives White the follow-up move at A.

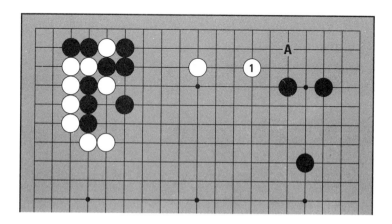

" Taking more side star regions than your opponent is one of the easiest roads to success in the opening. "

2. RUSH TO PLANT YOUR FLAG

Diagram 4.

The first four moves are all on corner star points. Next Black plays on the right side star point with 5. White plays a **knight's approach** at 6, Black answers, and White takes the upper side star point. Where do you think Black should play next?

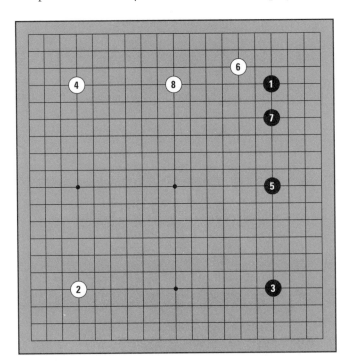

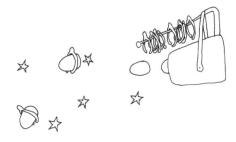

Diagram 5.

Suppose Black protects the right side at 9. White plays another side star point at 10, Black solidifies again with 11, and White takes the last side star point at 12. In this position, White has the advantage, because Black has stones on only one side, and White played first on all the others. You may remember from previous volumes that this isn't good opening strategy.

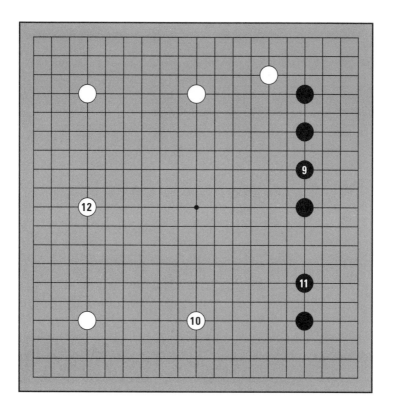

Diagram 6.

After White 1, Black should rush to play in a side star region. (These were called the "big points" of the opening in previous volumes.) Either Black 2 or a move at A is good.

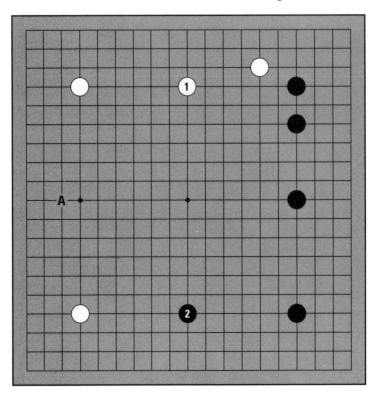

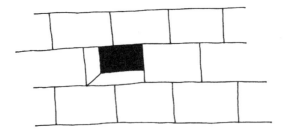

" Having thickness (a.k.a. influence or power) is useful when chasing weak stones. "

3. DRIVE TOWARDS YOUR THICKNESS

Diagram 7.

White **invaded** Black's area, then jumped out at 1. On the left, Black has a lot of thickness. Because of this, Black has the advantage here.

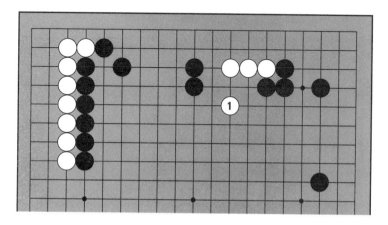

Diagram 8.

Black **caps** at 2, blocking White's escape into the center. If White plays the **diagonal** at 3, Black can give chase with the push at 4 and the **knight's move** at 6. White can **jump** at 7, but these stones are in trouble when Black continues the attack at 8, because they're running into a wall. Even if the group lives (a result very much in doubt), it will cost White a lot. Driving weak stones towards your thickness like this is a good strategy.

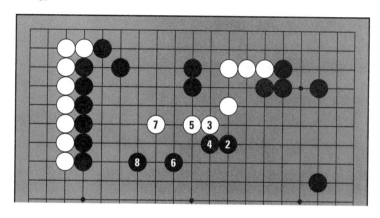

" Many times stones are killed because cutting points are overlooked. Unless you're planning on making a donation to your opponent, always make sure your stones can't be cut. *"*

4. STAY CONNECTED

Diagram 9.
Black plays 1, believing that the stones on the right are all connected, but Black's shape has a big weak point.

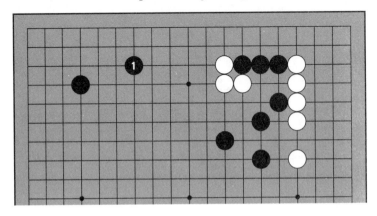

Diagram 10.
Black thinks these stones are connected because if White tries to cut at 2 Black can play at 3, connecting with the **tiger's mouth.**

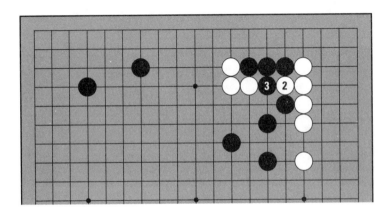

Diagram 11.

But Black has overlooked the clever move at 2. If Black connects at A, White can cut at B, and if Black connects at B, White can cut at A, so Black has inadvertently donated the three marked stones.

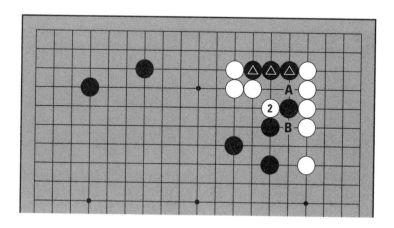

Nie Wei-ping 9 dan chooses for color on Korean television.

" *A mistake about life and death is often the biggest you can make. Check your groups carefully and often.* "

5. WATCH YOUR VITAL SIGNS

Diagram 12.
Is this white group alive?

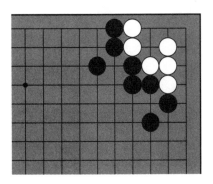

Diagram 13.
If Black plays the **hane** at 1, White can make two eyes at 2.

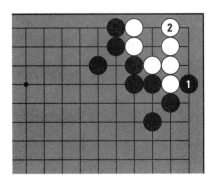

Diagram 14.
But if Black plays at 1 here instead, White can't live. (Notice that Black 1 threatens to capture two stones in a snapback at A.)

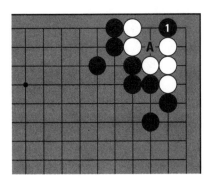

Diagram 15.
If White protects at 2, now Black can play the hane at 3, and White can't make two eyes. Because of the move at Black 1, the white group in *Diagram 12* isn't alive yet.

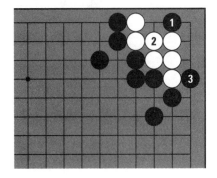

" As many top scorers on school tests know, don't sweat the unfathomable. Look around for easy ways you can add territory."

6. MINIMUM EFFORT, MAXIMUM PROFIT

Diagram 16.
In this position, there's a really big move that Black ought to grab. Where would you play?

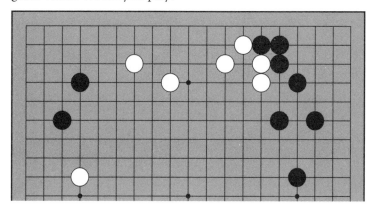

Diagram 17.
Black should play at 1, making a big territory in the corner. Let's see where he played instead.

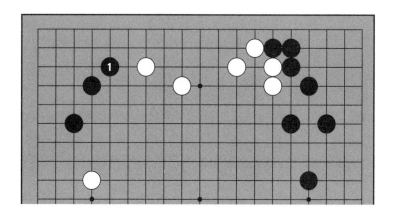

Diagram 18.

Black played at 1. But this move is just subtracting a point of territory—if he doesn't play, White can't possibly break in or live here anyway. Even if you're not absolutely certain whether Black 1 is necessary, you can figure that reducing your uncertainty to zero is probably not the most effective use of a move. After Black has wasted a move at 1, White can play a big move at 2.

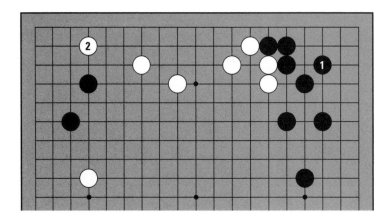

☾ TAKING MOVES BACK

You sometimes see people taking moves back, even though this is against the rules. Once you put your stone on the board, you can't change your mind. Save move changes for the analysis afterwards. You'll often find your first thought to be the better one anyway.

A common "takeback" situation arises during **ko** fighting. One side plays a **ko threat,** and the other side chooses to win the ko rather than answer the threat. Some people want to go back at this point, to play a ko threat that their opponent will answer. Not only should you not feel obligated to go back, it's impolite for your opponent to even suggest it. In professional go, taking back a move results in an automatic loss.

" *There is an objective standard for judging moves. Good moves make territory, increase your thickness, stabilize groups, and so on.* **Vulgar** *moves do this for your opponent, so they should be avoided. This may seem obvious, but nevertheless many people are tempted to play a move that they know is theoretically bad but seems not to hurt, or appears to offer some advantage. Sometimes you may not be able to resist playing a vulgar move or a move that is bad style, but remember: the more vulgar moves you make, the harder it is to win.* "

7. STYLE COUNTS

Diagram 19.
In this position, White has a cutting point.

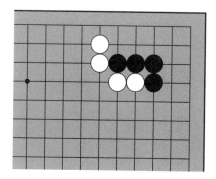

Diagram 20.
Suppose Black peeps at the cutting point at 1. White connects at 2. Black 1 is unspeakably vulgar, allowing White to protect the weak point, stabilize these stones and increase her thickness.

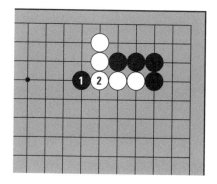

Diagram 21.
If Black is going to play here, he should cut at 1 and fight. Now that White's stones are cut, they are weak and can be attacked.

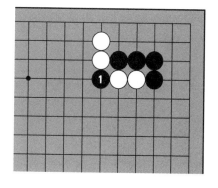

Let's look at another example of a vulgar move.

Diagram 22.
Black 1, "pushing from behind", is a vulgar move that helps stabilize White's stones.

Diagram 23.
Suppose Black pushes again at 3, White extends again at 4, and Black continues to push with 5, 7 and 9. Black has actually forced White to make a lot of territory.

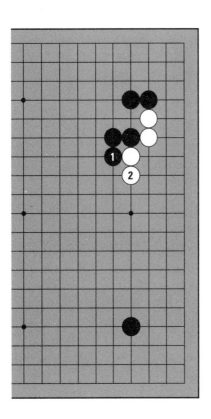

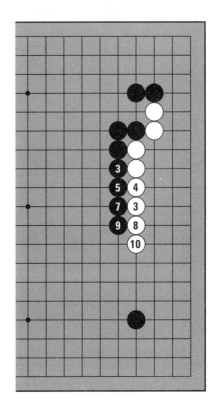

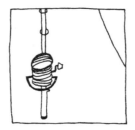
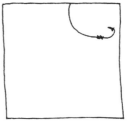

Diagram 24.

Protecting a weak point never goes out of style. (Do you see how Black 1 prevents White from pushing in and cutting?) Next, if White doesn't make a base at A, Black can play a sharp attack at B.

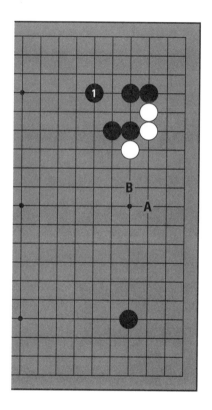

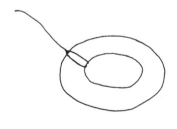

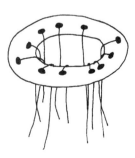

> "*A group's base is its area for making two eyes, and its territory is the surrounded area it controls. If the base is infiltrated, the territory is lost.*"

8.   HOLD THE LINE

Diagram 25.
In this endgame position, White has played at 1. Where should Black play?

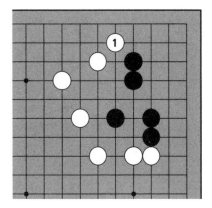

Diagram 26.
Black has to block at 2 to keep his base. Next—

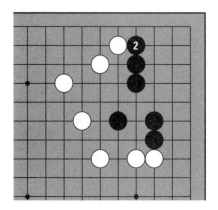

Diagram 27.
If White plays the hane, Black blocks. White connects at 5 and Black connects at 6. (It's also possible to play 6 at A.) The borderline here is completely determined now.

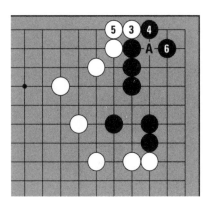

Diagram 28.
When White plays ⊚, if Black doesn't answer, White can jump in the corner. Now Black's group doesn't have a base and has to worry about living. Black's hard-won corner territory is destroyed.

② elsewhere

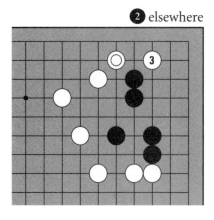

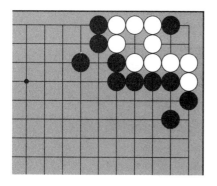

Diagram 29.
This position looks finished, but Black has an interesting move here. The corner looks like White's territory for sure, but Black can make **dual life.**

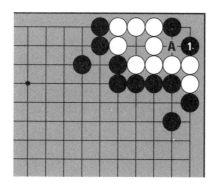

Diagram 30.
Black can play at 1. This is dual life, because neither side can play atari at A without putting him or herself in atari, so neither side can capture the other. In dual life, neither side has any territory. This area is not counted, but left as it is at the end of the game.

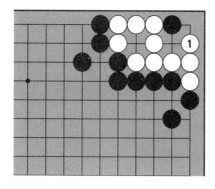

Diagram 31.
If White plays at 1, White gets the corner territory. Counting the one dead black stone, White has five points.

Ma Xiao-xiun 9 dan of China (left) vs. Lee Chang-ho 7 dan
of Korea in international competition.

Ma Xiao-xiun 9 dan vs. Cho Hoon-hyun 9 dan of Korea
(left) in a later round of the same tournament.

PART TWO

REAL GAMES

Part II analyzes three real games: A professional game, a nine-stone handicap game, and a pro vs. amateur three-stone handicap game.

Try to follow along with your own board and stones.

REAL GAMES

« A game of go has three stages: the opening, the middle game (or fighting stage), and the endgame. Let's look at an even game in the contexts of these three stages.

This game is between two professionals, Lee 4 dan and Jeong 5 dan. Lee 4 dan is Black and so must give five and a half points of compensation. In other words, White will receive five and a half points at the end of the game to compensate for Black's advantage in having the first move. »

OPENING

Taking the Empty Corners

It's easiest to make territory in the corner, so an even game usually begins with players taking the empty corners first. Black plays the "double star point opening." White plays one star point and one **3-4 point,** the two most common moves for taking empty corners.

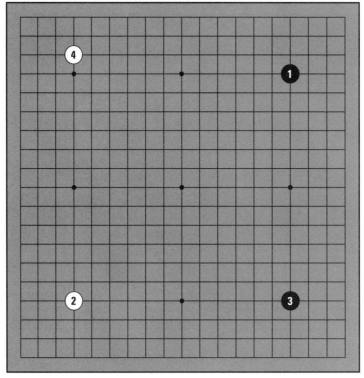

Game Record 1 (1-4)

Black Approaches

After taking the empty corners, playing in the side star regions is good strategy. However, you may decide to **enclose** your corner or **approach** your opponent's corner first. With 5, Black plays the **one-point approach** to White's stone on the 3-4 point. White **attaches** at 6, Black plays the hane at 7 and White pulls back with 8. White has made some territory in the corner with this sequence.

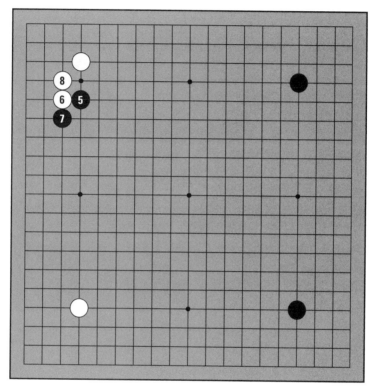

Game Record 2 (5-8)

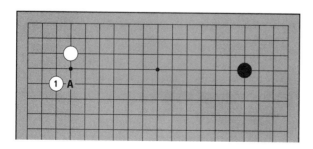

Diagram 1. As you may have seen in Volume II, from a 3-4 point, the corner can be enclosed with just one move. If Black doesn't play an approach, White may play the **knight's enclosure** at 1 or the **one-point enclosure** at A.

Taking the Lower Side

Black approaches another corner at 9, leaving the two stones in the upper left corner for now. White answers with the knight's move, and Black takes the side star point at 11, making a territorial **framework** on the lower side. If White cuts at A, Black plans to take another side star point at B.

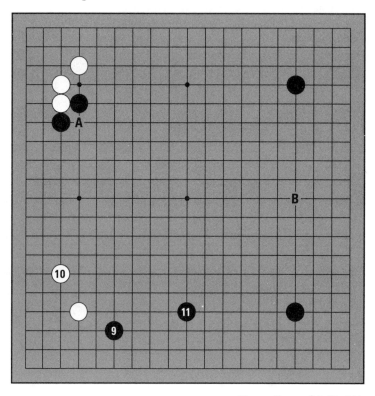

Game Record 3 (9-11)

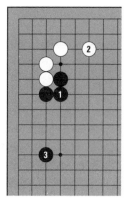

Diagram 2. Instead of 9, Black may connect at 1. White jumps at 2 and Black plays a **three-point extension** at 3. This is a **standard sequence.**

The Kite

White approaches the lower right corner with 12, since if Black takes the right side star point, Black will make a really huge framework. The one-point jump is the most common reply. The moves up to 16 are a common star point standard sequence, hereafter referred to as the "kite".

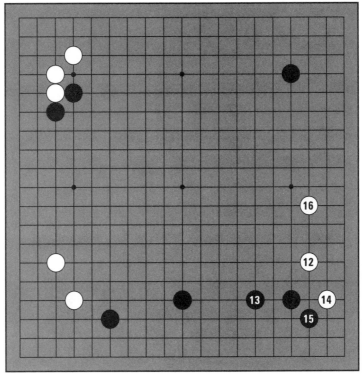

Game Record 4 (12-16)

Diagram 3. Instead of 13, Black may also choose another sequence, such as attaching on top at 1 and making a strong position on the lower side.

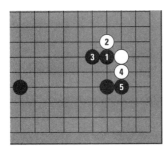

Diagram 4. The **pincer** at 1 is another possibility. If White jumps out at 2, Black keeps the pressure on while once again staking out a position on the lower side with 3.

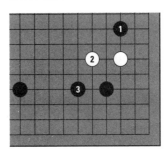

Deciding the Left Side

It's Black's turn to play, so he takes advantage of this opportunity to connect at 17. He then plays 19 according to the proverb about **extensions:** "If one, jump two; if two, jump three". White solidifies the lower left corner with 20.

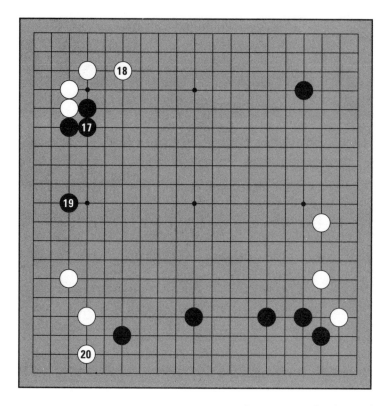

Game Record 5 (17-20)

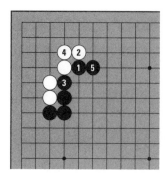

Diagram 5. White 18 in the game prevents Black from attaching at 1 here, then making thickness with 3 and 5 while flattening White in the corner.

Invading Black's Framework

White ◎ is a dual-purpose move: it solidifies the corner territory and aims at an invasion of Black's framework on the lower side. But Lee 4 dan chooses to ignore White and plays an enclosing move in the upper right corner at 21, so White jumps in at 22. This is the invasion point of Black's framework. What will happen next?

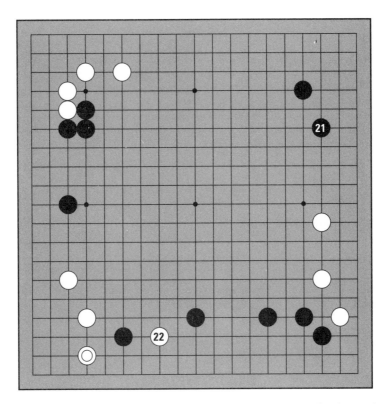

Game Record 6 (21-22)

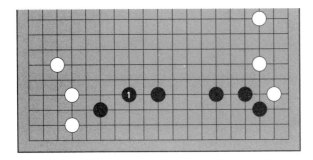

Diagram 6. If Black chose to respond on the lower side instead of playing 21 as in the game, he could strengthen his framework at 1.

Building a Wall

Dealing with this invasion is a bit difficult. Black attaches at 23, trying to seal off the center. White makes a base with 24-28. When Black plays at 29, what should White do? The way out is blocked, so White must live inside.

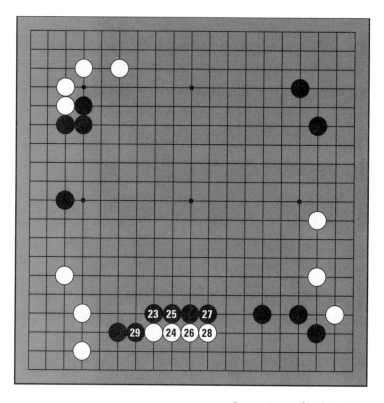

Game Record 7 (23-29)

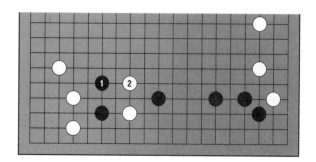

Diagram 7. Instead of 23, if Black jumps out at 1, White can follow at 2. Now it looks as though Black invaded White's area.

White Lives

White **slides** under Black's stone with 30, making a base for the group. When Black prevents the tiger's mouth at 31, White protects at 32. White can make at least two separate points of territory now, so the group is alive. Black's territory has been destroyed in the sequence up to White 32, so the invasion was a success.

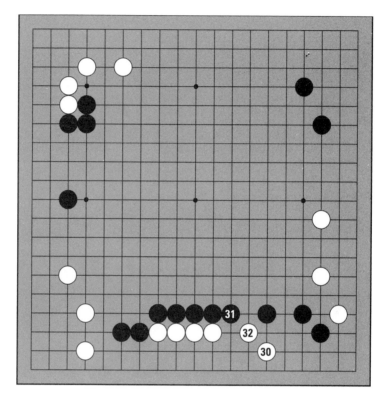

Game Record 8 (30-32)

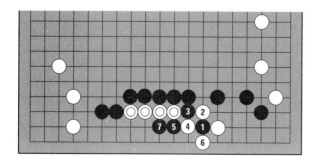

Diagram 8. White 32 is necessary. If there's no stone there, Black can lay a trap with 1 and catch the four marked stones in the sequence to Black 7.

Surrounding the Center

When your territory is destroyed you may feel a keen sense of loss. However, Black hasn't really failed. While White was struggling to live, Black was making lots of thickness in the center. If Black uses it well, the result shouldn't be bad for him. With 33-37 Black leans on White's group on the right side.

Black's strategy is to make territory in the center. Center territory must be protected on all four sides, so this is not easy. However, if White tries to destroy this potential territory by jumping in, Black can use his thickness in the center to mount a scary attack.

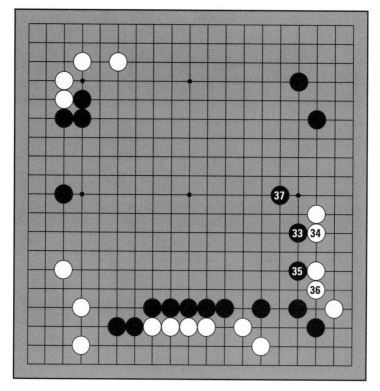

Game Record 9 (33-37)

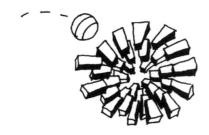

Barricade

White tries breaking through at 38. Naturally Black blocks at 39, since if he doesn't play here, White can come out at 39 and neutralize the center. White 40 peeps at the tiger's mouth. Black connects, and White plays atari at 42.

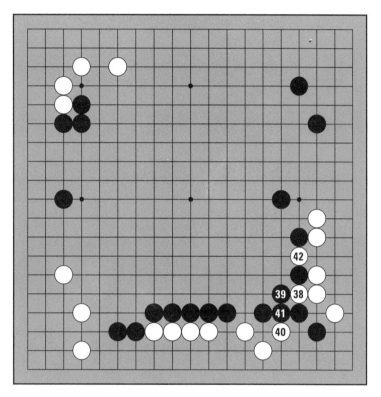

Game Record 10 (38-42)

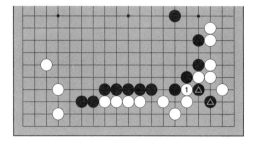

Diagram 9. If Black doesn't connect at 41, White cuts at 1 and Black is in big trouble—the two marked stones are dead and the whole corner becomes White's territory.

The Last Big Point

When White plays atari, Black doesn't connect but blocks at 43 instead. White captures at 44 and Black blocks again at 45, sacrificing one stone. Trading one or two points to block off the center is a pretty good exchange. Sometimes one must sacrifice a little to accomplish one's goal.

    White plays atari at 46 and Black connects at 47. Now White could capture a stone at A, but he grabs the side star region at 48 instead. You can see how valuable White 48 is if you put a black stone here and compare.

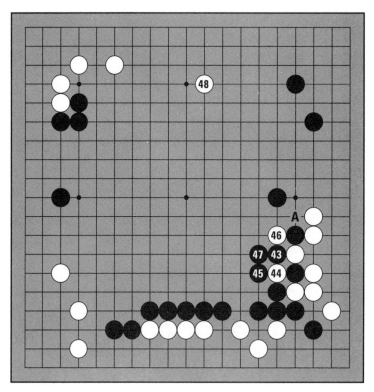

Game Record 11 (43-48)

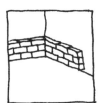

Solidifying the Corner

Black encloses the corner with 49. As you may remember from Volume II, after playing the star point and the knight's enclosure, you can solidify the corner territory with one more enclosing move at 49.

When White invades at 50, Black blocks at 51 and White can't live. White makes this exchange anyway, planting a **sleeper**—to use a term borrowed from espionage— a stone strategically placed for possible activation later. White 52 has two meanings: extending the territory on the upper side, and making the sleeper potentially more useful. At this point the opening is finished. The middle game fighting comes next.

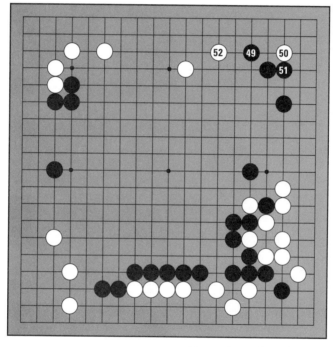

Game Record 12 (49-52)

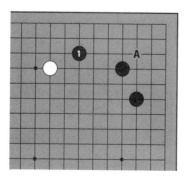

Diagram 10. Instead of 49, Black could try to make a bigger territory by playing at 1, but then White could probably mount a successful invasion in the corner later. For example, a **3-3 point** invasion at A is very difficult, often impossible, to kill. A position like this is said to have **potential** (*aji* in Japanese and *maat* in Korean).

MIDDLE GAME

THE MIDDLE GAME IS THE FIGHTING STAGE. CONTINUING WITH
THE GAME—

INVASION & ATTACK

Black jumps in at 53. White has a lot of territory, so Lee 4 dan is worried that if he
doesn't invade here, this may be a losing position for him.

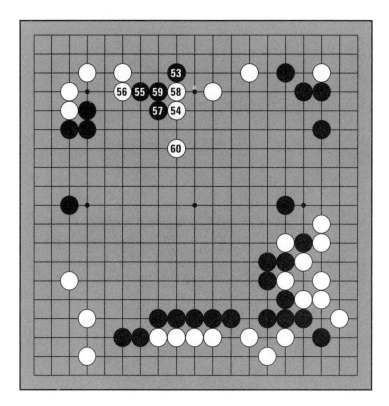

Game Record 13 (53-60)

Diagram 1. But what do you think of this: instead of invading at 53, Black plays at 1, White 2 protects the upper side, Black 3 pushes, White 4 extends, and Black 5 makes a knight's move? Playing for the center like this is called the "outer space style." Black has made a fairly impressive structure in the center. It's anybody's guess where White should play next.

This is a pretty good plan. Black 53 allows White to attack at 54, neutralizing some of Black's thickness in the center, which is the main thing Black has going in this game. On the other hand Black 53 is understandable, because it prevents White from making even more territory. Lee 4 dan agonized between these two options. Even long after the game, his internal debate continued.

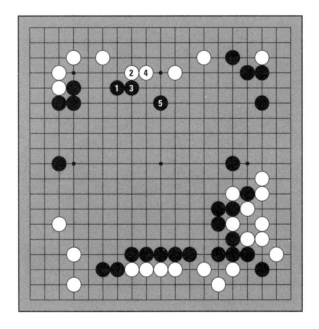

B. D'AMATO

If White could actually kill the invasion at Black 53, that would be a tremendous advantage for White and Black 53 would be a hideous mistake. But planning on killing is a little like planning to win the lottery. White wisely doesn't try to kill, but gets a good result by just coming out into the center while attacking. If you hear yourself starting to think about killing in your own game, run it by Reality Checkpoint #1: you probably don't have the grand prizewinning ticket. *Don't try to kill unless you read out exactly how it's going to happen.*

Black Knows White's Strategy

When Black extends at 61, connecting at 62 is the correct move. If White doesn't connect, Black can push in at 62 and cut. Black 65 is essential. Black needs to surround the center to stay in the game.

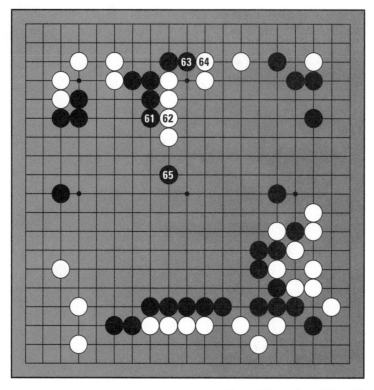

Game Record 14 (61-65)

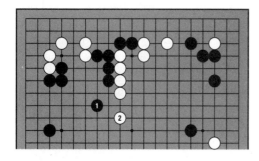

Diagram 2. Instead of 65, if Black comes out with the knight's move at 1, White plans to play the one-point jump into the center with 2. White has a lot of territory, so destroying Black's center area should lead to an easy win.

The Cut

After Black ⬤, it's difficult for White to get into the center. White attaches at 66. Black cuts by playing the hane on the inside at 67. If Black had played the hane on the other side at A, White would have come out into the center with B, seriously reducing Black's area. When White **crosscuts** at 68, Black extends at 69. This powerful way of playing, intending to cut off and catch White 66, is possible because Black has a lot of thickness. How can White answer the cut?

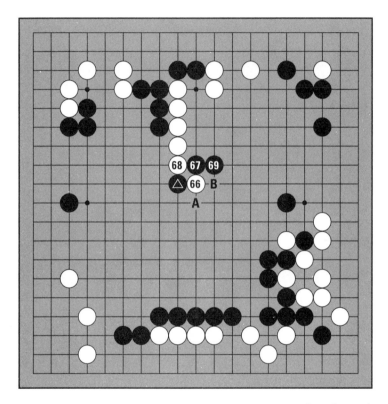

Game Record 15 (66-69)

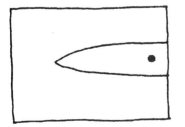
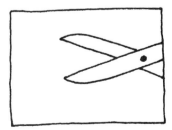

Giving Up One Stone

After Black cuts, White would like to strengthen his stone in the center, but has no choice but to give it up. First White exchanges 70 for 71 (a subtle way of creating cutting potential), uses the stone in the center to get the main force out with 72, and then makes a **tiger's mouth connection** at 74.

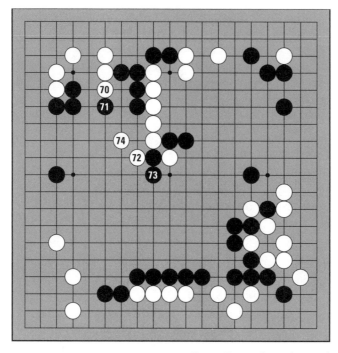

Game Record 16 (70-74)

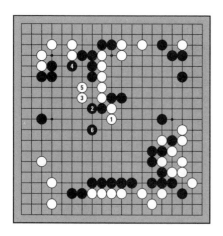

Diagram 3. Instead of 72, if White extends at 1, Black extends at 2. White's group on the upper side needs to come out with 3 and 5. If Black then jumps at 6, White's two isolated stones in the center are almost dead because of Black's surrounding thickness.

Black Makes Center Territory

Black 75 prevents White from playing there, and next cutting off the eyeless marked stones by playing at A or B. White 76 means to reduce Black's territory in the center. Black blocks at 77, and White extends with 78. After Black 81 the center territory is nearly complete. Black suddenly has made about thirty points here, so now the score is very close.

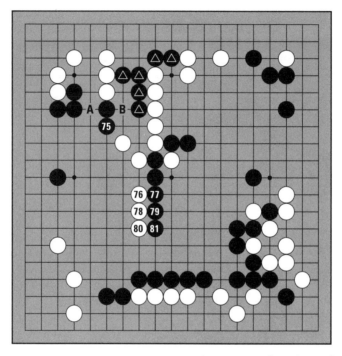

Game Record 17 (75-81)

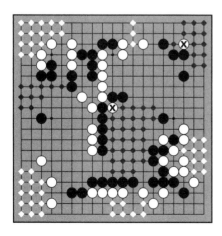

Diagram 4. Let's count how much territory each side has. White's upper left corner and Black's upper right corner are about the same, fifteen points each. Black's territory on the left side and White's territory on the right side are also about the same, ten points each. White's remaining territory in the lower left corner, on the bottom, and whatever White gets on the top, compared with Black's territory in the center, will decide the game.

Blocking the Cut

To the experienced eye, the borders are almost complete, and the middle game is
nearly over. White plays at 82, threatening a cut at 85, so Black protects with a tiger's
mouth at 83. White attaches at 86 and Black extends at 87. White 86 prevents Black
from playing A, White B, and then cutting at Black C. After 86 Black can't cut (try to
confirm this for yourself).

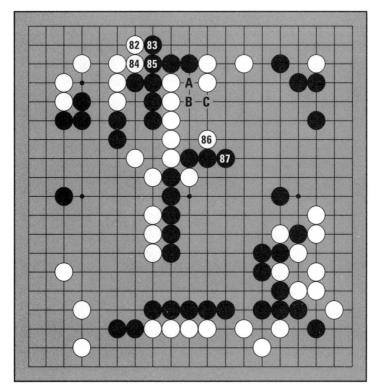

Game Record 18 (82-87)

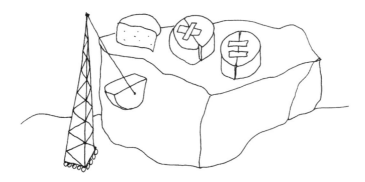

The Sleeper Awakens

After thinking for ten minutes, Jeong 5 dan attached at 88, activating White ◎. Planting the sleeper earlier didn't cost White anything, and now he makes a little territory on top while reducing Black's corner – a skillful bit of microwarfare. Black 89 is the only move.

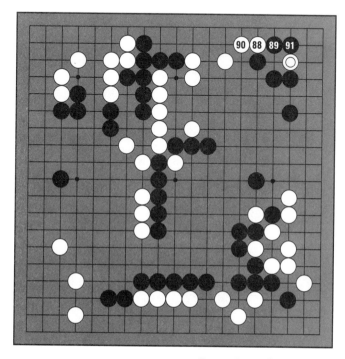

Game Record 19 (88-91)

Diagram 5. When White attaches, if Black plays the hane on the other side at 2, White pulls back at 3, Black has to connect at 4, and White can live in the corner with 5 and 7.

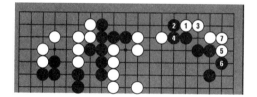

Diagram 6. If Black omits 91, White can **cross under** with 1 and 3.

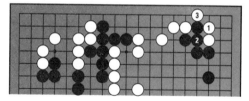

To the End

The big battles of the middle game are over, so the players move on to the endgame. It's White's turn, so he takes this opportunity to play 92. This move assures the capture of Black ⓐ. Black blocks at 93, and White plays the one-point jump at 94. This is a narrow extension, but it is quite large at this stage of the game, and there's a good follow-up sequence for White. Black prevents the follow-up by playing against the white stone at 95, and White quickly takes another large point at 98.

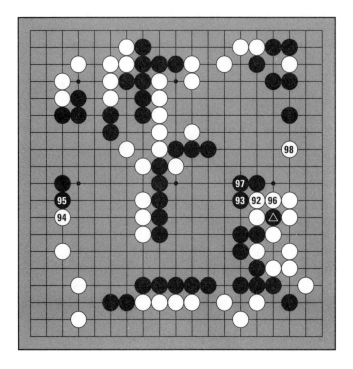

Game Record 20 (92-98)

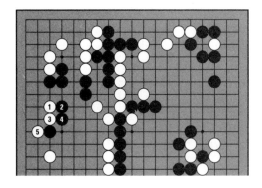

Diagram 7. If Black doesn't play 95, as a follow-up to 94 White can invade at 1, taking away Black's territory on the upper left side. Having a follow-up like this is one reason why moves like White 94 are big.

THICKNESS

The goal is always the same—make more territory than your opponent. How you achieve this is a more complex matter. There are two basic ways of making territory: you can try to surround it directly or you can use the indirect method of making territory while attacking. This second technique can be very effective, since in the competition to grab more points, you'd like to be playing big moves while your opponent is making small ones. In a good attack your moves will increase your territory (or reduce your opponent's) while he's busy just trying to make two eyes.

"Thickness" is essential to an effective attack and to the indirect method of making territory, but it's difficult to define. As with the concept of *sente*, what's thick or not is somewhat dependent on the skill of the players. For instance, a move might really be sente—that is, your opponent ought to answer it—but he's also free to play anywhere he likes. If he doesn't answer, was your move sente? By the same rationale, if your opponent is busy scrambling to make life because he's heard rumors about your formidable attacking skills, does that mean your position is thick? As you improve, you'll learn to recognize real sente and real thickness more and more accurately, gliding towards the "truth" until you are very strong and able to identify them correctly—most of the time.

A thick position has several attributes. To have thickness, stones should be connected and face some relatively unsettled area where they can exercise their influence. Then, when you attack, you drive your opponent's weak stones towards your thickness, something like the way cowboys might herd livestock into a corral. As your opponent's weak stones run up against your strong ones, you then make territory (or more thickness) on the other side of the "cowboy" stones. Another related technique is to build a big framework out of thickness—a structure so large that your opponent can't let you have it all but must invade. Then, once again, you go on the attack.

Thickness is like an investment—it's not cash in the bag, but if it's well-managed it'll leave you with more in the end than just hoarding money. On the other hand, if you make a mistake, you may not see a return, or worse, lose principal. Using thickness well means to take advantage of the fact that your opponent must make safety moves where you are thick. If you can't force him to do this or make him pay the consequences, your thickness isn't a good investment.

ENDGAME

THE BORDERLINES OF TERRITORY SKETCHED IN THE OPENING AND MADE IN THE MIDDLE GAME WILL BE COMPLETED IN THIS FINAL STAGE.

ENDING

Black plays the hane at 99, and White blocks at 100. Black plays atari at 101, and White connects at 102.

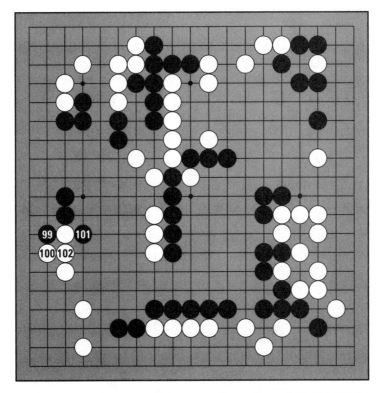

Game Record 21 (99-102)

Protecting the Upper Left Corner

Black comes straight down at 103 and White blocks at 104. When Black plays at 105, White must connect at 106. (Do you see why?)

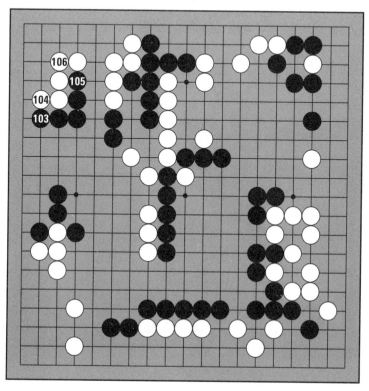

Game Record 22 (103-106)

Diagram 1. Black 103 is big endgame: if it were White's turn to play, he could play the hane at 1 and connect at 3.

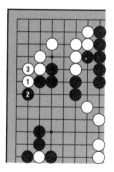

Diagram 2. If White doesn't play 104, Black quickly slides in at 1 or A, significantly reducing White's corner.

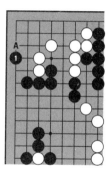

Finishing the Lower Side

Black still has the initiative, so he turns to the lower side and plays the sequence from 107 to 111. Black means to reduce White's territory and finish up this area. White 112 threatens to cut a diagonal, so Black connects at 113. White plays the hane at 114, Black blocks, and White connects at 116. Black leaves the cutting point at A for now and plays at 117, threatening to capture four white stones by cutting at 120. White 18 protects the cutting point with a tiger's mouth. Black plays atari at 119 and White connects at 120.

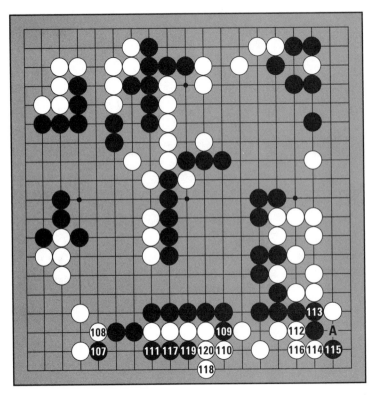

Game Record 23 (107-120)

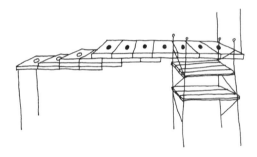

Black Waits For a Chance

Black connects at 121, preventing White from cutting there and catching one stone. Not only is this a big move, but Black has a nasty follow-up planned. White is aware of Black's plot and so answers at 122. Black finally comes back to connect at 125.

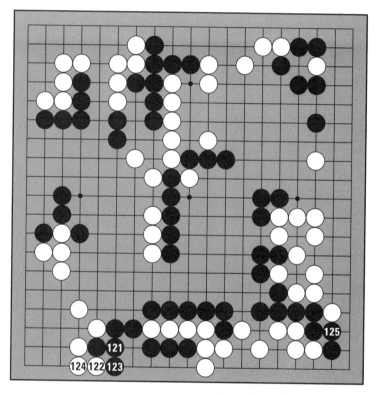

Game Record 24 (121-125)

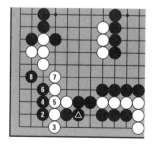

Diagram 3. If White omits 122 and cuts at 125 instead, Black can use the marked stone to **clamp** at 2 and invade White's corner with the sequence to 8.

A Nimble Ending

White plays the diagonal at 126 in sente: because Black needs to answer at 127, White retains the initiative. White 128 and 130, capturing one stone on the second line, is worth about ten points. Black 131 expands the territory on the left side while threatening to sever the three marked stones in the center from White's group on the upper side.

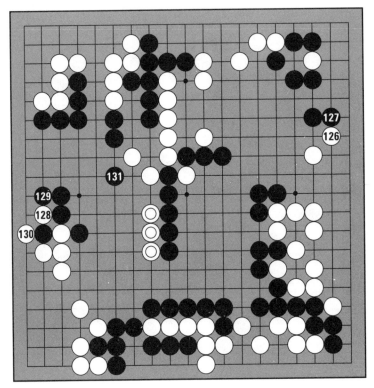

Game Record 25 (126-131)

It's a bit complicated to determine the exact value of an endgame move. Basically one adds what one side gains to what the other side loses to come up with a relative value. This method will be explained fully in future volumes; for now, the important thing to come away with is that big endgame moves:

1. are usually near the edge
2. increase your territory while decreasing your opponent's
3. ideally are sente or threaten big follow-ups
4. should be grabbed as quickly as possible.

Protecting the Cut

When White's group pushes out at 132, Black threatens a cut first with 133 and then blocks at 135. Black 135 is necessary to prevent White from driving a **spike** into Black's territory on the left. White 136 protects the cutting point at A. Watch your cutting points and make sure your groups are stable in the endgame; when you are focusing on territory, it's easy to blow the whole game with a single oversight.

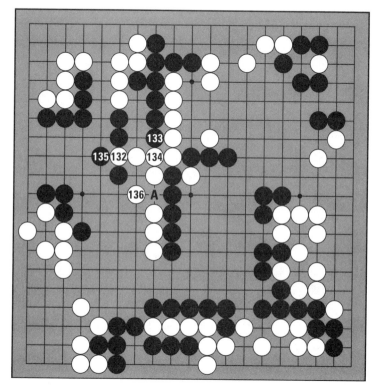

Game Record 26 (132-136)

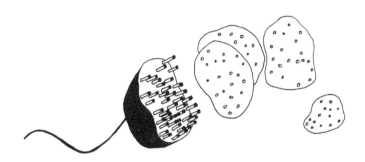

White's Advantage

The atari at Black 137 is sente. White has to connect at 138. Black cuts and captures a stone with 139 and 141. This is worth about eight points. White takes the initiative and plays the hane at 142. This is called **reverse sente,** because if Black had played here, it would have been sente for Black (i.e., White would need to answer). While playing this move, White believed that he would win. Jeong 5 dan counted that he had about fifty-eight points and Black around sixty points. Black is ahead on the board, but remember White gets five and a half points of compensation, so actually he is ahead by about three and a half points. But perhaps White should have protected at A instead of playing at 142.

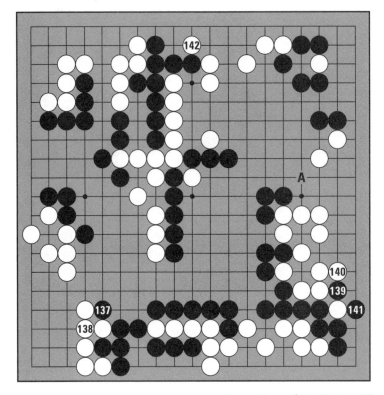

Game Record 27 (137-142)

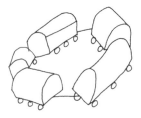

An Endgame Fight in the Center

Knowing the situation looks bleak, Black decides to attach at 143. Black's intention is to try to make a little territory here and reverse the game. When White plays the hane at 144, Black answers at 145. When White connects at 146, Black pushes in at 147. Black 149 connects in response to White's atari at 148. White has to connect at 150, and Black cuts at 151.

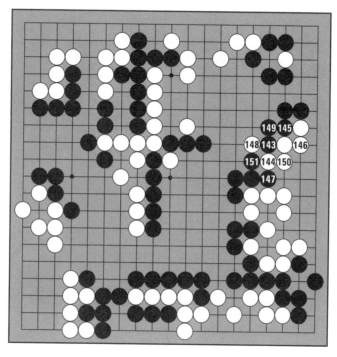

Game Record 28 (143-151)

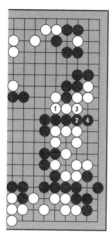

Diagram 4. Instead of 150, if White connects at 1, Black can drive in a spike with the sequence to 4.

Black's Territory Balloons

White extends at 152. This aims to reduce Black's territory in the center, and to increase White's territory on top. When Black plays a hane at 153, White plays one at 154, and when Black plays a **double hane** at 155, White plays one at 156. Black needs to extend at 157, White plays atari at 158, and Black connects.

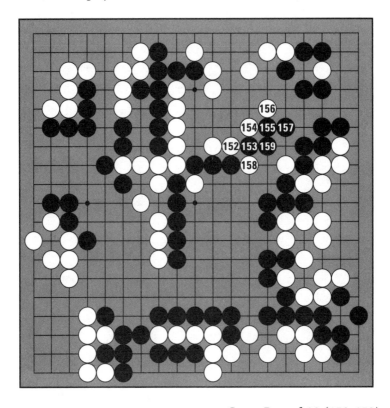

Game Record 29 (152-159)

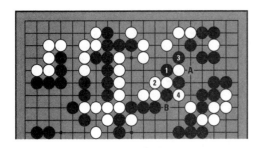

Diagram 5. Instead of extending at 157, if Black plays atari at 1 and tries to catch one stone with 3, White 4 is double atari. Black can capture at A, but White can destroy more territory than he loses with the capture at B, so the exchange is to Black's disadvantage.

Hane on the First Line

White plays a hane on the first line at 160. Usually Black would just block at A, but here Black **throws in** a stone at 161. (At the end you will see how the throw-in reduces White's **liberties,** preventing him from pushing at A and later forcing him to connect inside his own territory.) White captures at 162 and Black pulls back at 163. White connects at 164, since if Black cuts at 164 and White connects at B, Black can catch one stone at C. Next Black plays a hane on the first line at 165. Where should White respond?

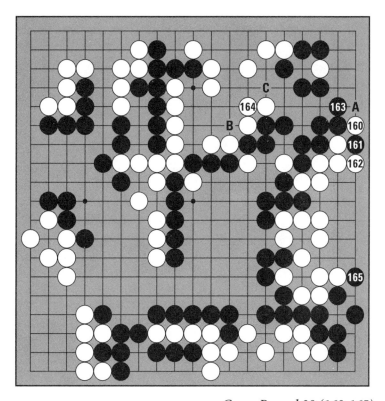

Game Record 30 (160-165)

The Correct Answer

White 166 is the best reply. Black extends at 167, hoping to make a little annex to the center territory, but White rushes in with the knight's move at 168, preventing him from doing so. Black expands the territory on the left side at 169. White reduces Black's territory in the center with 172 and 174.

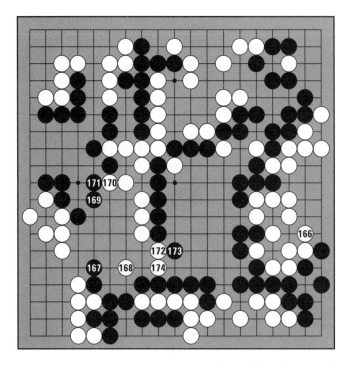

Game Record 31 (166-174)

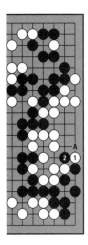

Diagram 6. Instead of 166, if White blocks at 1, Black can cut at 2 and the position becomes ko. If Black were to win this ko by capturing at A, White's side would be destroyed. This ko is too troublesome, so White avoids it by extending.

A Little Sente Before Blocking

White needs to answer both when Black threatens a cut with 175 and when he pushes in at 177. Next, Black is worried about weak points in the center, so he takes the time to **connect solidly** at 179. When White pushes in at 180, it looks like Black needs to block at A, but he plays 181 and 183 instead.

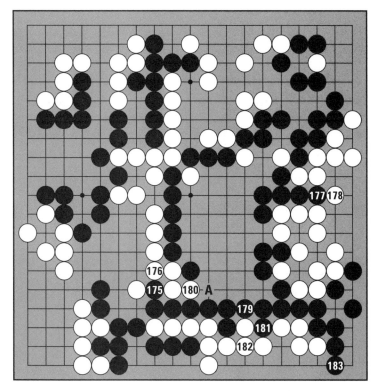

Game Record 32 (175-183)

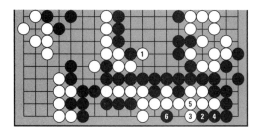

Diagram 7. If White ignores Black 183 and bursts into the center territory with 1, Black's attachment at 2 is big trouble for White's group on the lower edge. If White blocks at 3, Black can play atari at 4 and then strike a killing blow at the center with 6.

Magic

White must play at 184, so now Black can go back and block at 185. Next White plays a sequence of **sente endgame** moves. Notice that it is necessary for Black to answer White's cut at 192 by making two eyes at 193.

At this point Black has sixty-seven points. White has sixty-one points, two captures that Black can dispute by ko, plus five and a half points of compensation. It looks like it will be a half-point game, but suddenly White pulls a rabbit out of his hat. Lee 4 dan yelped with dismay at his oversight when White jumped into his left side territory at 194. Black can't catch the invader because White is able to cross under at A or B.

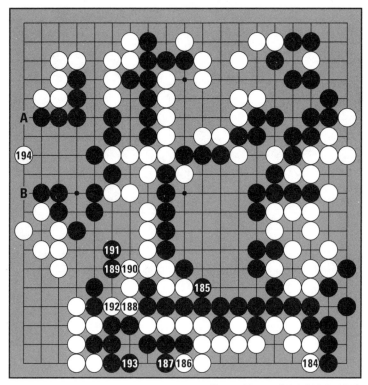

Game Record 34 (184-194)

Estimating the score during the game is called **positional judgement** or just **counting.** To do this well you need experience. Not only can it be difficult just to count points and keep track of them, but there's a certain amount of predicting the future involved as you try to determine where the boundaries of incomplete territories will be. Sometimes it's not even clear which stones are alive and which are dead. For now, try to count the areas where you think each side has made territory by drawing imaginary lines completing the territories and see how close your estimate is to our judgement. Precise counting methods will be discussed at length in future volumes.

White's Victory Is Assured

White crosses under in the sequence to 200, reducing Black's territory on the left side considerably. Now only small endgame moves remain. With 194, what was an extremely close game became certain victory for White.

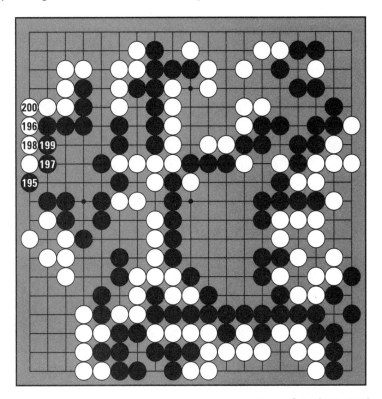

Game Record 34 (195-200)

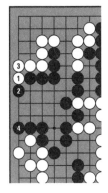

Diagram 8. Instead of 194, Black expected White to play the hane at 1 and connect at 3. Then Black would have played straight down at 4, making four points more than in the actual game.

Extra for Experts: It's not exactly a four point loss, because in this sequence it's now White's turn to play, but in the actual game, after White crosses under it's Black's turn. But in this case it's more than enough to seal the game for White.

Small Endgame

Black pushes in at 203 and protects at 205. (Do you see why Black 205 is necessary?) White pushes in at 206, Black blocks at 207, and White blocks at 208.

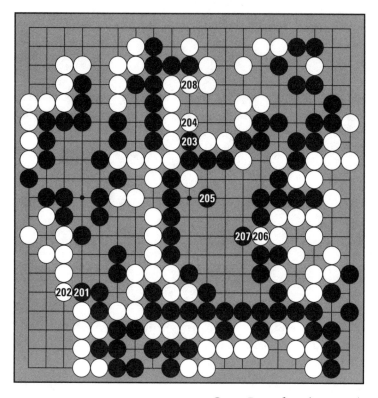

Game Record 35 (201-208)

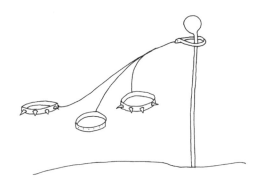

Finishing the Upper Side

Black plays the hane at 209, White blocks, and Black connects. White protects at 212. Black attaches at 213, and White blocks at 214. Black has something nasty planned if White ignores 215; White needs to answer with 216. Next Black completes the border in the upper right, gaining a little bit of territory with 217 and 219. White's capture at 220 is a two-point endgame move.

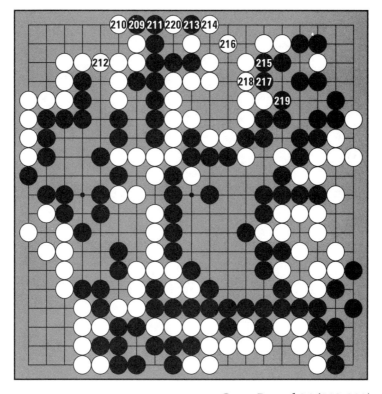

Game Record 36 (209-220)

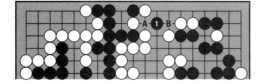

Diagram 9. If White plays elsewhere with 216, Black can play at 1, threatening two cuts at once at A and B.

The Game Is Over

Black 225 makes one point. White 226, 228, 230, and 232 are all one-point sente endgame. Connecting at 236 is unavoidable because of Black's earlier throw-in at 161 (where White 240 is in this game record). After White connects at 238, a ko at 240 remains, but Black doesn't have enough ko threats to fight and win this ko, so he fills in a **neutral point** with 239. White connects at 240, and the game is over.

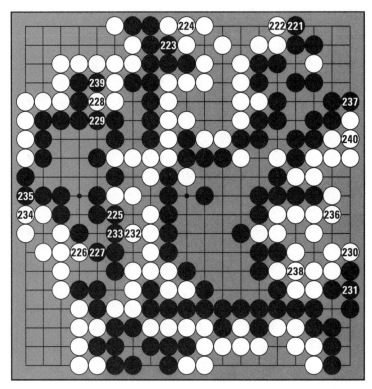

Game Record 37 (221-240)

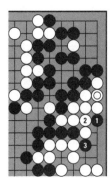

Diagram 10. White can't connect at White ◎ without playing 236 first; otherwise, Black can **pin** eight white stones at 1 (if White connects at 2, Black cuts at 3). Also, note that for the same reason, there's no chance for White to push in at Black 237 in the game record.

The result is a three-and-a-half-point win for White. Even though Black is actually two points ahead on the board, five and a half points of compensation make White the victor. Most professional games are quite close, and are decided within the bounds of the compensation.

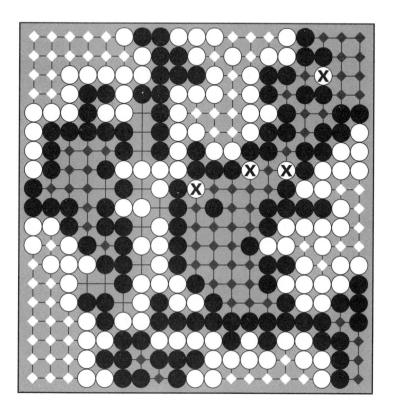

Black		White	
left side	11	upper left	15
lower side	2	lower left	18
lower right	4	lower side	6
center/upper right	40	right side	8
dead stones (4 x 2)	8	upper side	12
captures	1	captures	5
		compensation	5½
Total	**66**	**Total**	**69 ½**

6 A NINE-STONE HANDICAP GAME

HERE BLACK WAS A SEVEN-YEAR-OLD SIX KYU PLAYER. IN A HANDICAP GAME, THE WEAKER PLAYER BEGINS WITH SOME STONES ALREADY ON THE BOARD.

BLACK'S ADVANTAGE

In a nine-stone handicap game, Black has stones on all the star points. How big is Black's advantage? In experimental nine stone games between evenly matched professionals, Black wins by more than one hundred twenty points.

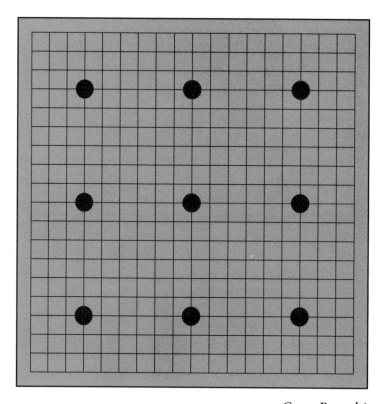

Game Record 1

GUERRILLA STRATEGY

White begins operations with the approach at 1. Black has already taken all the key points, so for all practical purposes there is no opening. This kind of game resembles guerrilla warfare—from the beginning, White jumps into Black's area and fighting begins. Black 2 is a calm answer to White's approach. When White plays 3, Black plays another one-point jump.

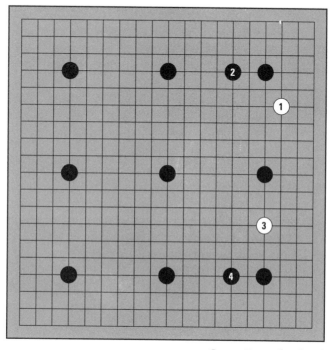

Game Record 2 (1-4)

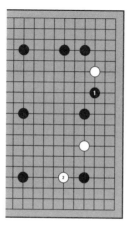

Diagram 1. Instead of the one-point jump at 4, if Black switches to 1, White 2 weakens Black's corner by approaching on both sides. The corner is the most important area, so in the game answering White 3 at Black 4 was a good idea.

THE CAP

White plays the cap at 5. This is an attempt to use the marked white stones to attack. White hopes to scare Black into thinking that the side star point stone is in trouble. Actually White's surrounding stones are very weak, so White should be in more trouble than Black. The one-point jump at Black 6 is not bad. Next White plays a one-point jump at 7.

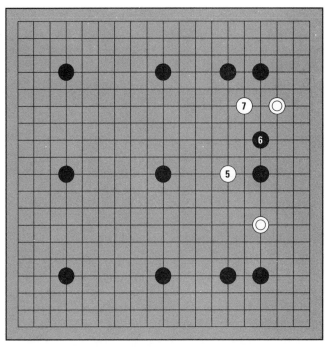

Game Record 3 (5-7)

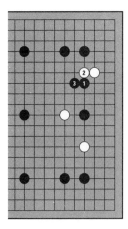

Diagram 2. With Black 6, there are many other ways to play. Leaning on White with the shoulder hit of Black 1 is one possibility. If White extends at 2, Black can extend at 3.

BOTH CAMPS MOVE OUT

When Black attaches at 8, White plays the hane at 9, and Black extends at 10. This is a good idea. You don't want your stones to get sealed in, so it's important to move out into the center. As an added bonus, as Black comes out, White's stones are split into two forces on the upper and lower right side. Since neither force has a base yet, both may be attacked. White jumps at 11, preventing Black from playing here and sealing him in. Black plays a strong cut at 12.

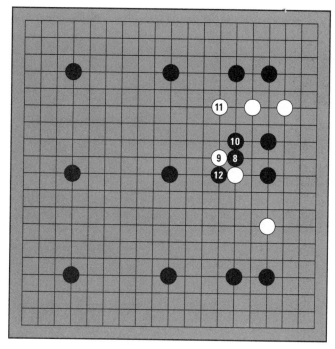

Game Record 4 (8-12)

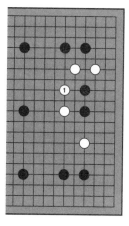

Diagram 3. If Black doesn't move out into the center, White could quickly seal in Black's two stones.

Quick-Change Artist

When Black cuts, White has to do some fast maneuvering with 13 and 15. Now Black is being surrounded.

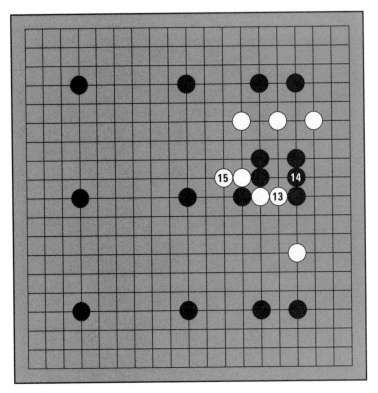

Game Record 4 (13-15)

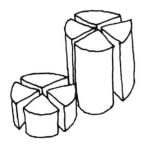

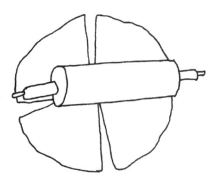

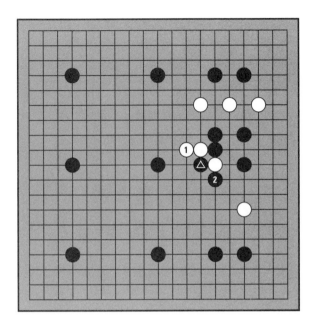

Diagram 4. White 13 is a sharp counter to the cut at Black ⊿. If White had just extended at 1, Black could have trapped one stone at 2.

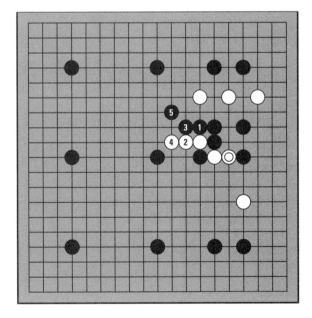

Diagram 5. An easy wasy to play is to ignore White ◎ and play atari at 1. Once Black's group has pushed its way out, White's group in the upper right becomes a target.

Black's Escape

White's weak point is a bit difficult to find, but Black hits it with a jeweler's precision. Black 16 is the optimal point for splitting the **large knight's move.** Black has also neatly escaped—White can't cut at A, because then Black could catch three stones at B.

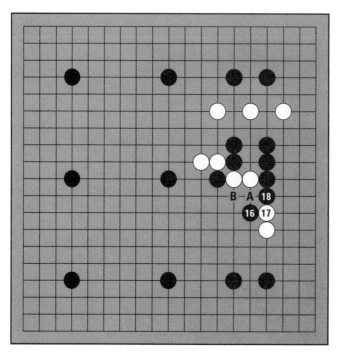

Game Record 6 (16-18)

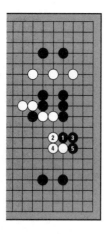

Diagram 6. Handicap stones make life easier. Black has a lot of help nearby, so even if he can't find the key, he can still negotiate these stones out of solitary confinement. For example, instead of 16, Black can attach at 1. White has to give way at 2 and 4, letting Black escape with 3 and 5.

A Vulgar Move

White plays atari at 19, and Black makes the vulgar exchange of Black 20 for White 21 before connecting. Notice the result is the same as if Black had just connected at 22 and then wasted a move at 20. White now has the time and the opportunity to focus on settling the stones in the lower right with 23.

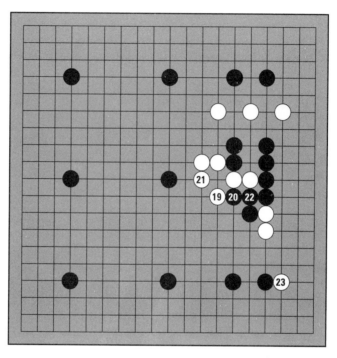

Game Record 7 (19-23)

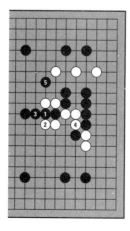

Diagram 7. Black also could have saved his stone by running at 1. Then if White pushes at 2 and cuts at 4, Black can slice White's forces in two and march out between them at 5.

A Calm Answer

With the attachment at White ◎, the game has become complicated. Black 24 is the correct side to play the hane. When White plays a hane at 25, Black connects at 26. Instead of Black 28, cutting at A is standard. White would connect at B, and Black would catch a stone with C.

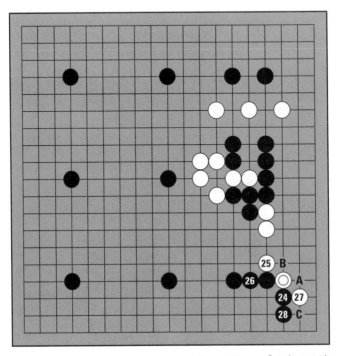

Game Record 8 (24-28)

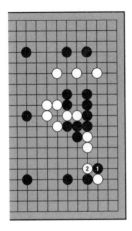

Diagram 8. With 24, if Black plays the hane on the other side, White plays the hard-to-deal-with cut at 2. While Black's hands are full in the corner, the big black group on the right side could be surrounded and killed.

A Frayed Rope

With White 29, Black's group on the right side looks like it has been surrounded, but White's stones are hanging together by a thread. Black doesn't even really need to worry about being surrounded, because there's room on the side to make two eyes. Black slashes through with the hane at 30. White cuts at 31, Black pushes in at 32, and White blocks at 33. When Black cuts at 34, White has to run at 35 and 37. Now Black's ten-stone group on the right side and White's six-stone group in the lower right are sealed in. Who will be killed?

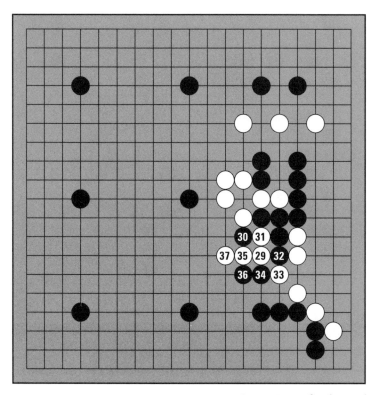

Game Record 9 (29-37)

A Sharp Attack

Black plays atari at 38 and cuts at 40, going for the kill. This is a serious problem for White. In desperate straits, White fakes an escape at 41.

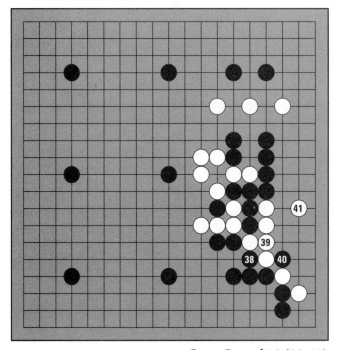

Game Record 10 (38-41)

Diagram 9. White doesn't have a good response to Black 40. Instead of 41, if White connects at 1, Black can play 2, 4, and 6. Since the captured Black ⬤ is a **false eye,** White will die. Instead of Black 2 in this diagram—

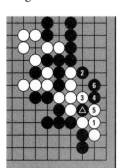

Diagram 10. Black can also play at 2 here. When White runs at 3, Black can capture White's stones in the sequence to 12.

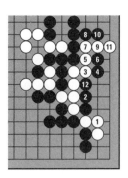

Falling For It

Attaching at Black 42 aims to prevent White from escaping along the side, but actually this is what White is hoping Black will play. White quickly **wedges** at 43 and connects at 45. Now White has made an **eye shape** of more than six points, which is enough to live. Black's chance has slipped by.

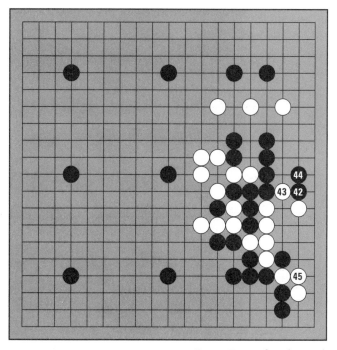

Game Record 11(42-45)

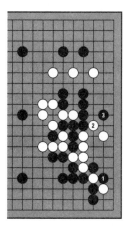

Diagram 11. Instead of 42, Black could have landed a mortal blow by capturing a stone at 1. Then even if White plays 2, Black 3 prevents White from getting out.

Making a Base

Since White is alive, Black's group is now in trouble. Black was disappointed about
not killing the group, but recovered his composure nicely and turned his attention to
the crisis at hand. Black 46 lays the foundation for making a base. When White plays
47, Black enlarges his **eye space** with 48 and 50. Black hates to play these moves,
because they practically force White to play 49 and 51, weakening Black's position in
the upper right corner. But if Black wants to live, he has no choice.

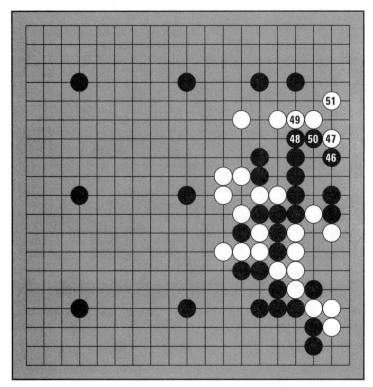

Game Record 12 (46-51)

Chilling Thoroughness

Is Black alive on the side? Black blocks the upper right corner with 52, thinking to protect the corner now that his group is alive. But this is mistaken thinking: Black doesn't realize that White can still attack his group. White attaches at 53, plays the tiger's mouth at 55, and extends at 57—before White plays the final blow, he wants to make his surrounding stones safe from counterattack. Black answers everything, unaware that White has read his mind and is calmly sealing the black group's fate.

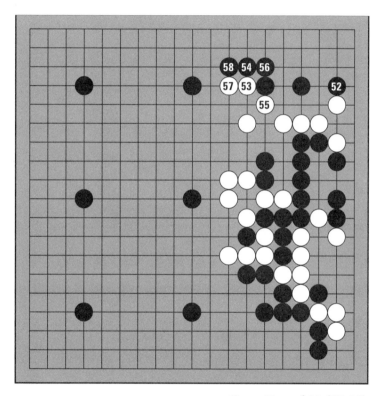

Game Record 13 (52-58)

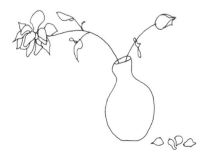

Black Dies

Finally White goes for the kill with 59. This hane reduces Black's eye space. Flustered, Black plays a simple atari at 60, and White just connects.

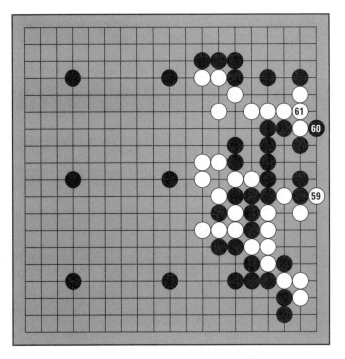

Game Record 14 (59-61)

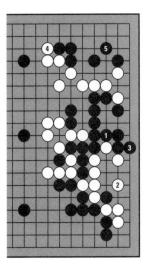

Diagram 12. Black could have saved his group by playing 1 and 3 instead of responding at 58 as in the game. Then even though White can seal the upper right corner group in by turning at 4, Black can protect these stones with 5. Once White plays at 59, the big black group on the right side is dead.

A False Eye

Caught off guard, Black struggles on, playing another atari at 62. This time White doesn't connect but plays at 63. Even though Black captures one stone at 64, this only makes a false eye.

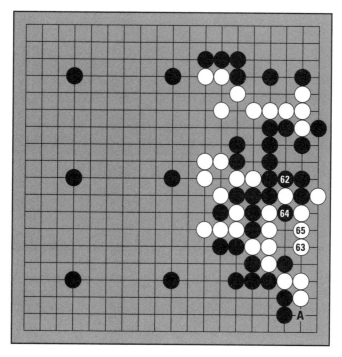

Game Record 15 (62-65)

④ ... ◎

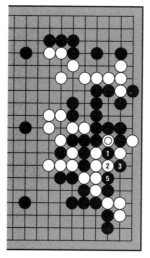

Diagram 13. If White omits 63, White will be in trouble when Black captures at 1. If he blocks at 2, Black cuts at 3. If he then captures one stone with 4, he still can't escape when Black plays atari at 5.

Extra for Experts: Can you guess why White didn't just connect but played at 63 instead? White realized that a stone at 63 kills Black just as well as connecting, and also keeps Black from making territory in the lower right corner by playing the forcing exchange Black A–White 63.

Major Success For White

Black tries to make a living eye shape by blocking at 66, but White can play the throw-in at 67. Then when Black captures at 68, White makes the killing move at the center of the **bent three.** Black needs two eyes to live, but White 69 makes this impossible. (Try to confirm that A and 67 are false eyes and Black is dead.)

Losing a group like this hurts. How big is the loss? There are twenty stones in Black's group. Killing twenty stones is the same as making forty points of territory, since in addition to the twenty points of territory White gets, the dead black stones will be used to reduce Black's territory by twenty points. This forty points plus White's other territory gives him a total of about sixty points.

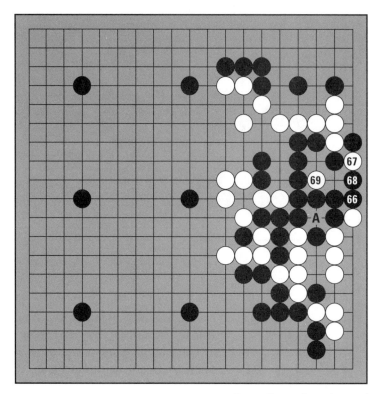

Game Record 16 (66-69)

Building the Upper Side

Black 70 aims to cut at 71 and start a fight. White prevents this by playing at 71, and Black plays an enclosing move in the upper left corner with 72. It's more common to play at A, but Black 72 is possible. White approaches at 73, and Black answers with the one-point jump at 74.

Black's calm assessment and play show a good attitude for go. Even though the group on the right was killed, Black is still not behind. White has sixty points, but Black has large frameworks on the upper and lower sides. The future fighting will determine the result. Next, when White jumps in the left side at 75, what's a strong response for Black?

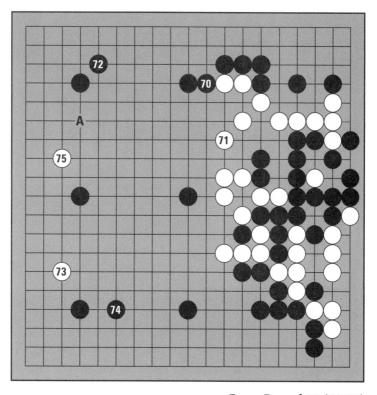

Game Record 17 (70-75)

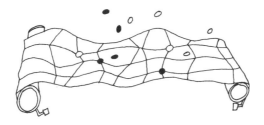

Opportunity Lost

Black caps at 76. This prevents the white stone from jumping out, but since White can make a base by attaching underneath at 77, Black 76 lets White off the hook.

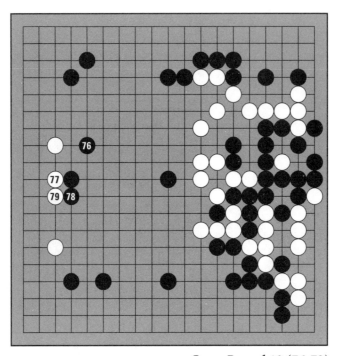

Game Record 18 (76-79)

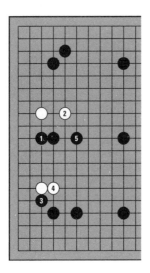

Diagram 14. Instead of 76, the **iron pillar** at 1 is good here. If White jumps out at 2, Black can play the diagonal attachment at 3 to make White's position on the lower left **heavy** (unwieldly and inflexible) and then jump to 5. Now two white groups are in trouble. For go players, attacking two weak groups is paradise, and having two weak groups is a nightmare.

Two Cutting Points

Instead of playing the hane at 80, Black should have just extended at 83. When White cuts at 83, Black has problems. In order for Black 80 to get out into the center, Black has to play atari at 84, but when White runs at 85, Black has two cutting points at A and B. Black can't protect these two weak points with one move, so Black 80 was a mistake. Now if Black connects one side, the other will be captured. Which side should Black save?

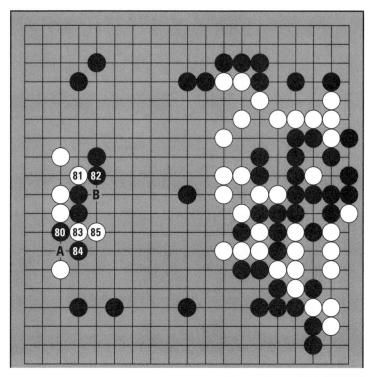

Game Record 19 (80-85)

Black Saves Two Stones

Black saves the two stones in the center by making a **knight's connection** at 86. It may seem better to save two stones rather than just one, but in this position it would have been bigger to connect the other cutting point.

When White cuts at 87 the left side becomes White's territory. Next Black tries to seal White in with 88 and 90.

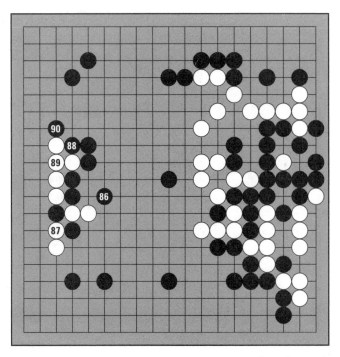

Game Record 20 (86-90)

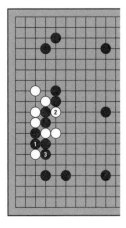

Diagram 15. Instead of 86, if Black connects at 1 and White cuts off two stones with 2, next Black can press down at 3, trapping one white stone. Since Black can make a lot of territory in the corner while preventing the left side from becoming White's territory, this sequence is better for Black than the one in the actual game.

Upper Side Territory

When White plays 91, Black extends at 92. White pushes at 93 and Black blocks at 94. White plays the two-point jump at 95, and Black makes about fifty points by protecting the top with 96, almost as much as White's territory on the right side. On the left White has fifteen points, but Black's lower side is much bigger. In a nine-stone handicap game, even if White kills a big group, Black can still win.

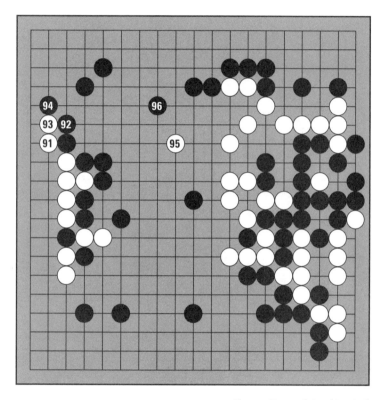

Game Record 21 (91-96)

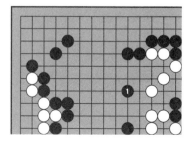

Diagram 16. If White omits 95, Black can complete the perimeter around this area with 1, making more than sixty points on the top half of the board.

The Endgame Begins

If he doesn't make a big mistake, Black can win this game. White comes into Black's lower side and lives fairly easily. Now the endgame begins, with White having the initiative. White makes a lot of points with the clamp in the upper right corner, and gets a big sente hane on the edge at 129. But Black has locked up a lot of territory, and is not giving up hope.

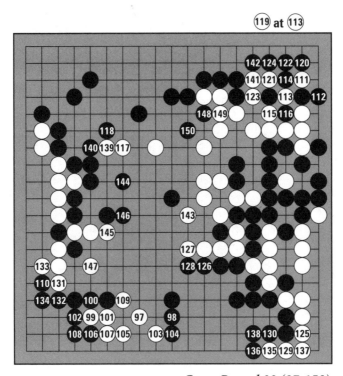

Game Record 22 (97-150)

Sente moves like White 129, the hane on the edge, are big because it doesn't cost a turn to play – Black has to block and then protect the cutting point to save any territory here, so White reduces Black's territory for free. The hane hitting the head of two stones is especially big because Black can't block directly at 135 (do you see why?)

Black Holds His Own

White has made up some ground in the endgame, but not quite enough. Black's good play on the lower edge gives White no points in this area. Can you count what the score is now? It's very close on the board, and in handicap games White usually receives no compensation.

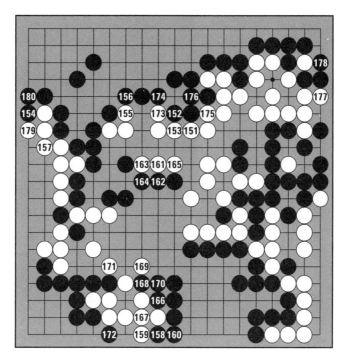

Game Record 23 (151-180)

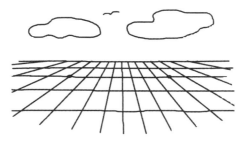

Wrapping it Up

Look around carefully in the microendgame – there are usually many plays that reduce your opponent's territory by a point, or ways of making a point of your own, hiding like little truffles.

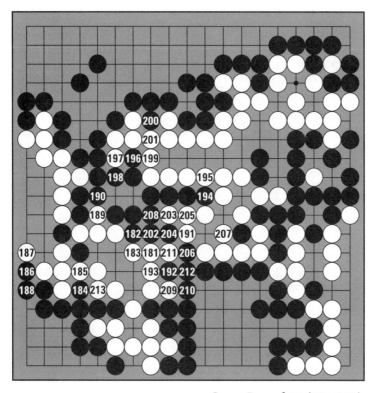

Game Record 24 (181-213)

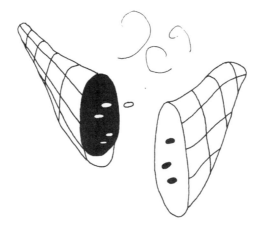

The Score

White 213 is the last move of the game. There are still some unplayed neutral points, but there are no more moves where territory may be made or lost. After a long struggle, Black has pulled off a one-point victory.

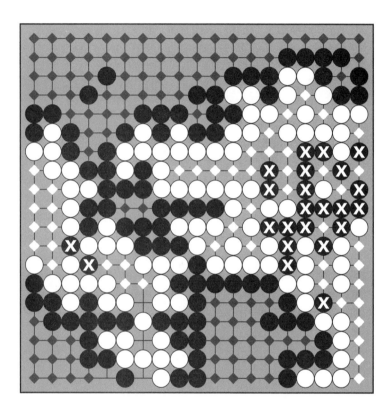

Black

upper side	61
center.	2
lower left	11
lower right.	21
captures.	_4
Total.	**99**

White

left/lower side	14
right side	34
dead stones (23 x 2)	46
captures	_4
Total	**98**

7 A THREE-STONE HANDICAP GAME

LET'S LOOK AT A THREE-STONE HANDICAP GAME, THE LEVEL AT WHICH BLACK, ACCUSTOMED TO LARGER HANDICAPS, MAY START TO FEEL A SIGNIFICANT PART OF THE ARMY HAS DESERTED. IN THIS GAME A PROFESSIONAL FOUR DAN GAVE AN AMATEUR FOUR DAN THREE STONES. ALTHOUGH THE TERM "DAN" IS THE SAME, THERE IS A GAP BETWEEN PROFESSIONAL AND AMATEUR RANKS.

A STANDARD SEQUENCE

One corner is empty, as are the sides and center. It looks pretty wide open, but Black still has a big advantage. White plays in the empty corner on the 3-4 point. Black approaches at 2. The pattern from White 3 to Black 8 is a standard sequence.

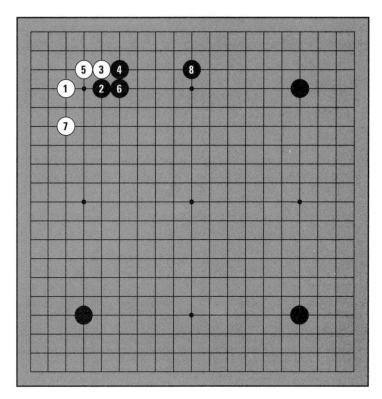

Game Record 1 (1-8)

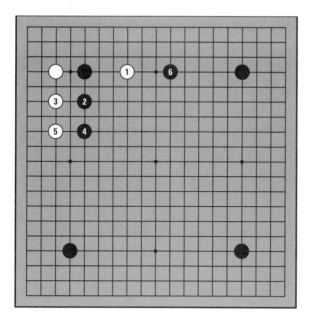

Diagram 1. Instead of attaching underneath at 3 as in the game, White can also start fighting early by playing a pincer at 1. Next Black can jump into the center with 2 and 4 and make a counter-pincer at 6.

  ## HOW TO IMPROVE

If you study Volumes I-III in this series, with a little experience your strength should be about ten to twelve kyu (in other words, you would receive about five handicap stones from the six kyu who played Black in the last chapter). If you have a lot of experience, you may be even stronger. Playing real games is probably the best way to improve, but if you want to make even faster progress, here's some time-honored advice:

1. Record your games.
2. Review and ask about positions you don't understand.
3. Let thinking, not emotion, guide your play.
4. Try what you learn.

Positive Moves

White plays the knight's approach to the star point stone at 9. The one-point jump of Black 10 is a standard reply. White makes a wide extension at 11. Black plays an enclosing move in the lower right corner and puts pressure on White's stones on the right side with 12, an example of killing two birds with one stone.

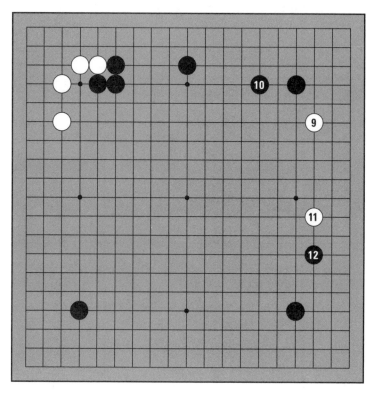

Game Record 2 (9-12)

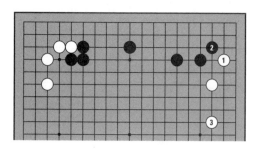

Diagram 2. With 11, usually White plays a standard sequence such as the kite. But in a handicap game, White must play more actively in order to counter Black's advantage.

Defiance

When White plays the knight's move at 13, Black jumps in with high spirits at 14, refusing to "play White's game" and answer in the corner as White envisions. White jumps at 15, Black jumps at 16, White 17 takes the corner, Black blocks, and White jumps again at 19. Because of Black 14 the situation has become very complex.

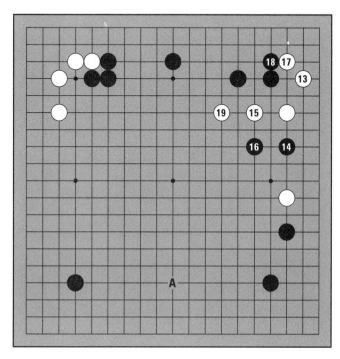

Game Record 3 (13-19)

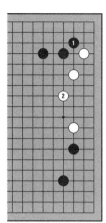

Diagram 3. Instead of 14, if Black answers at 1, White will protect with 2. Black can then seize the initiative, taking the side star point at A in the game record. This standard sequence is pretty good for Black, but there's something to be said for defying the opponent's expectations, even if they are reasonable.

Baiting

Black attaches under White's stone with 20. This stone is easy to capture, but White blocks at 21, not going for it. Black plays an exchange in sente and then caps at 24, a good attack on White's lone stone on the right side. White ignores this and invades the upper side at 25.

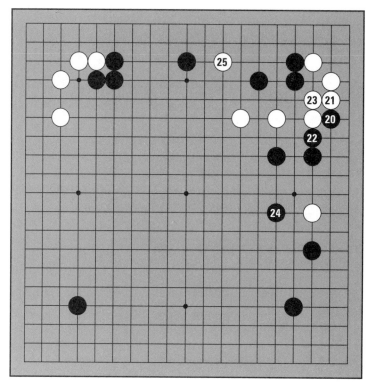

Game Record 4 (20-25)

Diagram 4. Instead of blocking at 21, if White goes for the bait with 1, Black cuts at 2. After White 3, Black can atari on top at 4 and connect at 6. White has caught one black stone, but the two marked stones are cut off.

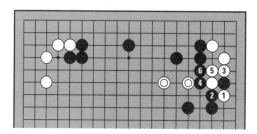

Another Front

White ⊚ aims to destroy Black's territory on the upper side. Blocking at 26 and 28 is the best Black can do—he has to let White live inside in order to stay connected. When Black extends at 30, White extends at 31, threatening to push in at A and cut off three stones in the corner. How should Black answer?

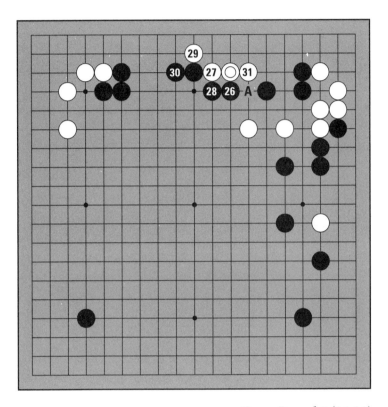

Game Record 5 (26-31)

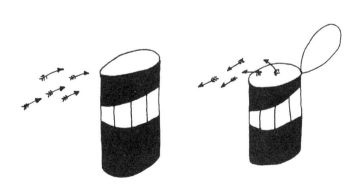

Living in Sente

Black needs to connect at 32. Next White makes a base with 33 and 35. White lives, so the invasion was a success, but Black has made some thickness and so has no complaints. Black 36 prevents White from crossing under at A, but since White is already alive, this move isn't so big. White gratefully takes the opportunity to make a fast exit at 37. Invading, living and having it still be your turn is like having it all.

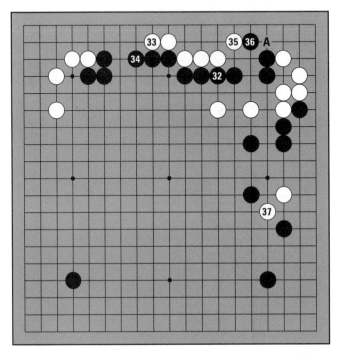

Game Record 6 (32-37)

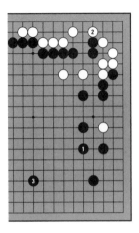

Diagram 5. Black 1 here, surrounding one stone, is bigger than 36. Black is happy if White connects underneath at 2 next—Black takes the side star point at 3.

Determining the Upper Right Corner

Black doesn't answer White ◎ but plays 38 instead. This move keeps the initiative, since White has to **descend** at 39 to live. Black 40 is also sente; White must protect at 41. Next Black turns at 42, making a little territory while threatening White's group in the corner. Even though Black's group is not surrounded, having a base will prevent a future attack. White blocks at 43, and Black plays atari at 44 and the hane at 46. Next, if Black connects at A, White's stones here can't make two eyes. What should White do?

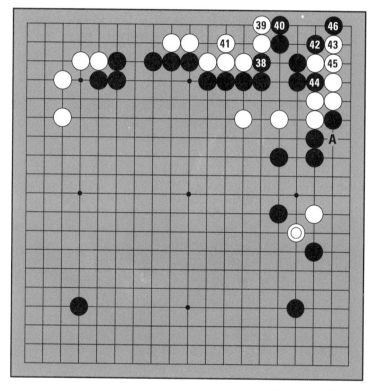

Game Record 7 (38-46)

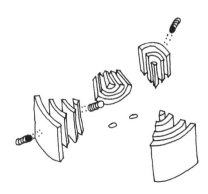

Attacking With Panache

White captures one stone with 47 and 49, securing life. This costs White sente, but eliminates a lot of potential problems. Black's initiative: the knight's move at 50 is a stylish attack.

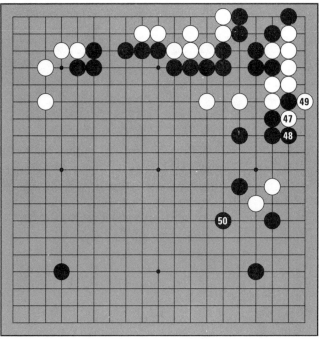

Game Record 8 (47-50)

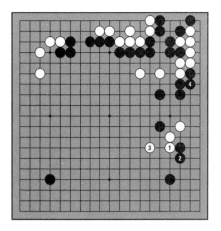

Diagram 6. If instead of capturing, White pushes at 1 and then comes out with 3, Black could connect at 4. Then White's big group in the upper right would be in trouble.

Pulling Out The Big Guns

Black ▲, following the proverb "attack with the knight's move," is right on target. It's difficult even for a professional to get away. White thought for several minutes before attaching on the far side at 51. When Black extends at 52, White plays the hane underneath at 53.

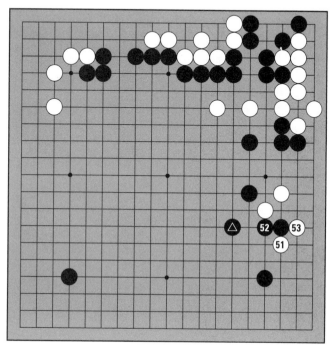

Game Record 9 (51-53)

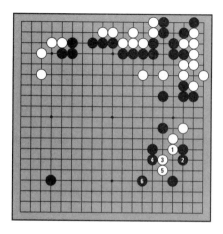

Diagram 7. Instead of 51, if White pushes at 1 and comes out at 3, Black can push at 4 and attack with the knight's move at 6. White doesn't have even one eye, so living is very difficult.

Trivia Note: go ranks and martial art ranks are calibrated on the same scale. Bruce Lee was a professional four dan martial artist.

The Meaning of the Attachment

White ⊚ is like the secret gadget hidden in the shoe that gets James Bond out of a tough spot. Seeing that he can't prevent White from oozing out the side, Black turns at 54. White extends at 55, Black blocks at 56, and White makes a base with the plays to 61.

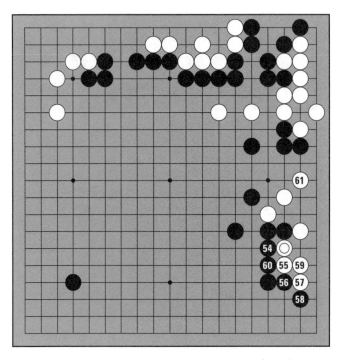

Game Record 10 (54-61)

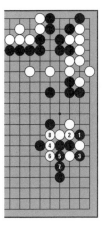

Diagram 8. Instead of 54, if Black had tried to cut at 1, White could cut at 2. Then if Black traps a stone with 3, White can come out by playing atari on top at 4 and 6 and connecting at 8, sacrificing two stones to break out.

Aiming to Kill

Black plays the hane at 62, atari at 64, and another hane at 66 to destroy White's base. White was quite surprised by this attack. When White plays atari at 67 Black connects at 68, and answers 69 at 70.

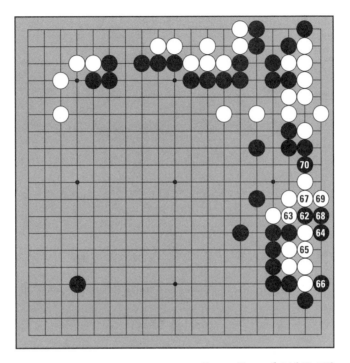

Game Record 11(62-70)

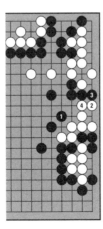

Diagram 9. If Black plays 70 somewhere else, at 1 here for example, White can live by playing at 2. Black has to block at 3 to prevent White from connecting, so then White can make a second eye with 4

Making an Eye

There is a proverb: Big groups don't die. (This should be sung to the tune of "Big Girls Don't Cry" by the Four Seasons.) Killing is not easy. White pushes at 71, Black 72 blocks, and White attaches at 73. When Black blocks at 74, White plays atari at 75. White needs to make a second eye, since capturing the black stones at A only yields one eye when Black plays at the **vital point** of the resulting bent three eye shape. Do you think White will be successful?

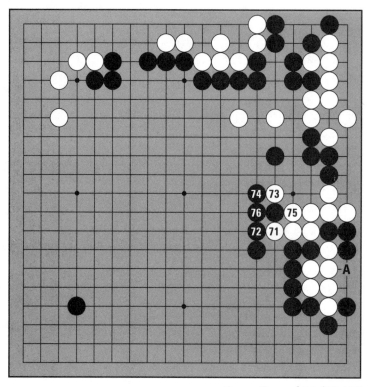

Game Record 12 (71-76)

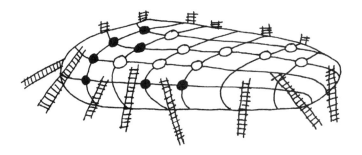

Big Groups Don't Die

The tiger's mouth at 77 is a good move. Next White can cut at A. Black wisely protects the weak point with 80, letting White makes the second eye with 81.

Even though Black fought valiantly, White's big group survived. But Black is also doing well. Black has the initiative and can take the big point at 82. White gave Black a lot of power in the center; using this power Black can make a big territory on the lower side. Also, Black has a clever move at B, which would cut off White's group in the upper right from the marked stone. Even though Black didn't kill, this attack gave him a big advantage.

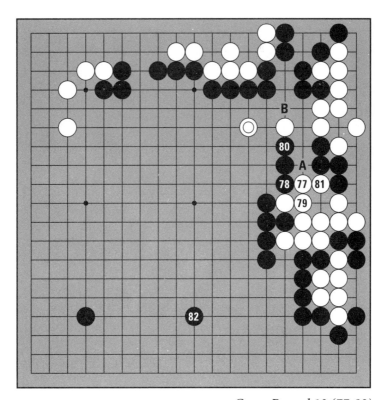

Game Record 13 (77-82)

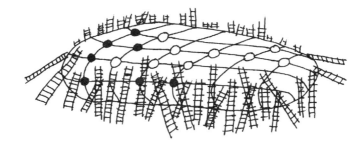

A Methodical Attack

White jumps in at 83. Black's area on the lower side is too big, so White must break in to stay in the game. Black 84, making an iron pillar, protects the right side and prevents White from making a base. White needs to escape into the center with 85 and 87, and Black chases him while making territory with 86 and 88. Black is attacking in a methodical, step-by-step way.

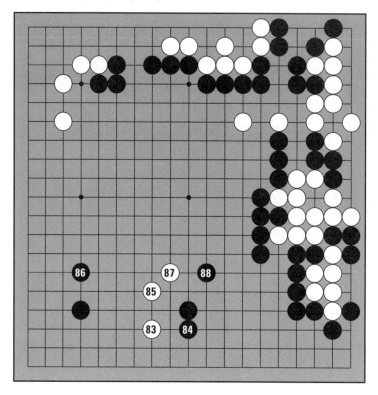

Game Record 14 (83-88)

Diagram 10. Black 84 is a good move. Capping at Black 1 would allow White to slide into Black's territory at 2.

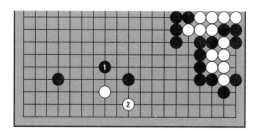

Black's Lead

White jumps again at 89. When Black peeps at 90, White must connect—if White doesn't answer, Black can push in and cut White's stones at 91. Next, Black continues to expand his area with 92. Increasing your potential territory while attacking is always a good idea.

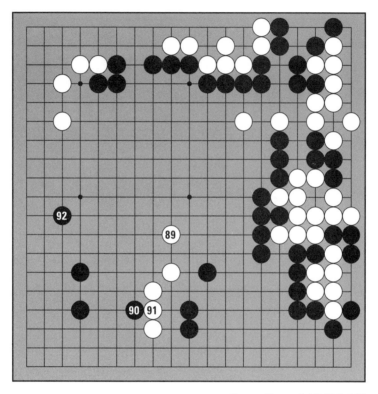

Game Record 15 (89-92)

B. D'AMATO

White is Resigned

White jumps again at 93, stengthening his group while trying to neutralize Black's thickness. Black peeps again at 94, then secures the corner territory with 96. White takes the last remaining extension at 97, but Black, who realizes he is far ahead, seals up the game by playing solid moves that assure him of at least twenty-five points in the lower left.

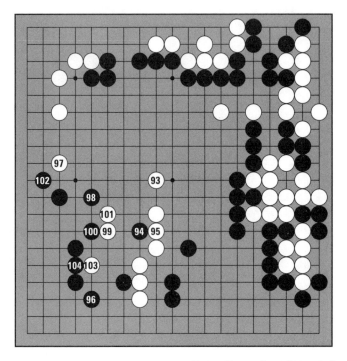

Game Record 16 (93-104)

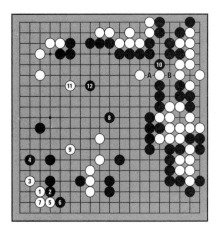

Diagram 11. Instead of jumping at 93, if White tries to prevent Black from securing the corner by invading at 1, Black's cap at 8 is harsh. White's big group can probably live, but Black make a big territorial framework in the center by cutting off a stone with 10 (if White A, Black cuts at B, and if White B, Black cuts at A, so White can't connect).

Final Score

By a conservative estimate, Black has sixty-six points. It looks like the White's maximum, including captures, is forty-three points, so Black is ahead by twenty-three points. White didn't see any hope, so he resigned.

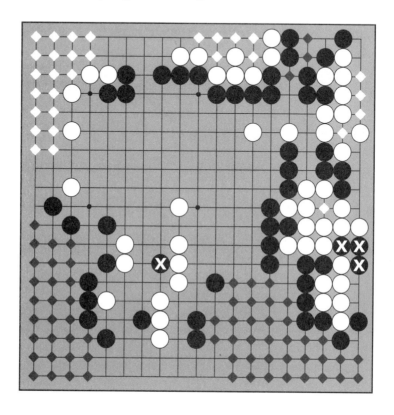

Black

lower left 28
right side .35
upper right 3

Total 66

White

lower right 1
upper right 4
upper side 6
upper left 19
center 4
dead stones (4 X 2) 8
captures 1

Total 43

THICKNESS II

The terms *thickness, influence,* and *power* are used somewhat interchangeably, although they aren't quite the same. The basic concept is similar, since each is useful for the indirect method of making territory while attacking. How they differ: thickness generally refers to outward-facing, connected groups, or in the endgame we might say one side is 'thick' to indicate she will have an easy time picking up more points because of the relative strength of her position. But a stone may have more influence or power than another because of its *location.* For example, a stone in the extreme corner has only two liberties, while one on the edge has three and one in the center has four. Since a stone with more liberties is harder to capture, the implication is that a stone in the center is more powerful. On the other hand, you only need two stones to surround a point of territory in the extreme corner (but three on the edge, and four in the center). We can extrapolate that it's easiest to make territory near the edges of the board, where stones are less powerful. Don't carry this to extreme conclusions, though. A stone on the edge itself is not the best for making territory, because it's just too weak. Neither is playing closer to the center always better, because at the end of the game you could find yourself with a lot of influence but not enough territory.

One way to visualize the board is not as a flat square, but as a pyramid with the center star point as its apex. The closer the stone is to the center, the higher it is on the pyramid. That's why we talk about playing closer to the center as playing **high.** Playing near the edges is called playing for territory, or playing **low.** It's important to maintain a balance—you don't want to play too high or too low. The **third line** from the edge is called the 'territory line', since it's an effective tier for making territory. The **fourth line** is called the 'power line', since it's a good height for gaining influence. Each line has a weakness—the third line can be pressed flat, and the territory can be scooped out from under the fourth line, but using these key tiers minimizes the drawbacks of playing low or high.

It's said that Lao Tzu was mainly an 'influence player', a style that can be hard to understand, and that Confucius was a more straightforward 'territory player'. My observation is that influence players tend to be more optimistic and may overestimate their position, and territory players are often conservative and may undervalue their assets. Or you may—as I do—combine the two styles, and over- or under-estimate your position with equal frequency.

Ma Xiao-xiun 9 dan begins a game.

Nie Wei-ping 9 dan analyzes after a game while engaging in a self-defeating habit.

8 | EVEN AND HANDICAP GO

PLAYING EVEN

Diagram 1. In this even game, both sides have played on the star points. This is a reasonable opening for both, but Black, by virtue of getting the center star point, has the advantage.

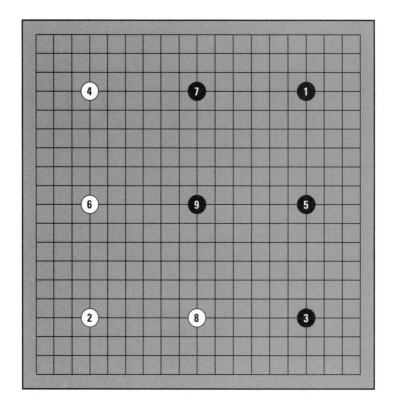

In an even game Black's advantage is counterbalanced by giving White compensation, usually five and a half points. For example, suppose that at the end of a game Black has seventy points and White has sixty-seven points. White gets an additional five and a half points for a total of seventy-two and a half points, so White wins by two and a half points. The half point is designed to prevent ties, since if the compensation were a whole number, both sides could have the same total at the end.
To make the game even, without Black having the advantage, first choose for color. This means the older player takes a handful of white stones, and the younger player guesses odd or even. Put down one or two black stones (instead of saying "odd" or "even") and choose whether you want Black or White if you guess correctly (it's usual with a 5 1/2 point compensation to just take Black). At the end of the game, add five and a half points compensation to White's total.

If one side is a bit weaker, that person can take Black and play first without giving White any compensation. Playing first without giving any compensation is called playing *seon* in Korean and *sen* in Japanese.

HANDICAP GO

If there is a bigger gap between two players, say of more than two kyu or **gup** ranks, they can still play using handicap stones. The weaker player places black stones on the board before the game begins, usually the same number as the gap between their ranks. Handicap stones are placed according to the following diagrams.

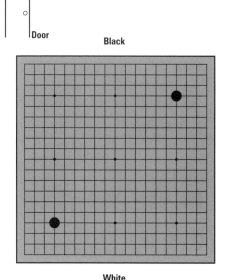

Door

Black

White

Two-stone handicap

A ten-kyu player may put two handicap stones like this against an eight-kyu player.

As a point of etiquette, the stronger player sits at the "front" of the board. The front is the side farthest away from the door, and the handicap stone closest to White should be placed on White's left side.

Three-stone handicap

Players with a three rank difference in strength between them may play a three-stone handicap game.

Black

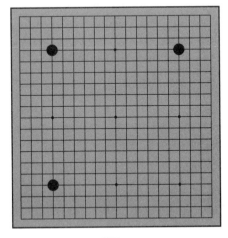

White

Once again, Black should put the handicap stone closest to White on White's left side. The idea here is that you leave the right corner in front of the stronger player clear for White's first move.

Four-stone handicap

A four-stone handicap, with stones in each corner on the star points, is the first of the high handicaps.

Five-stone handicap

An additional stone is placed on the center star point.

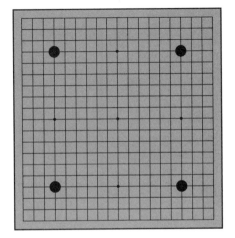

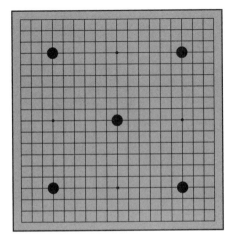

Six-stone handicap

The stone on the center star point is replaced by two stones on the side star points.

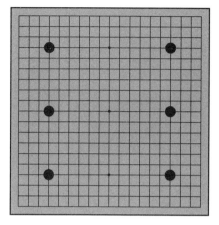

Seven-stone handicap

An additional stone is placed on the center star point.

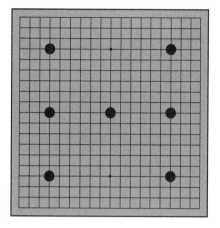

Eight-stone handicap

A ten-kyu player may put eight handicap stones, one on each star point except for the center, with a two-kyu player.

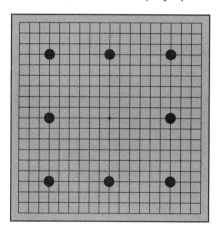

Nine-stone handicap

Black occupies all the star points on the board.

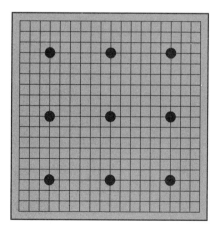

Handicaps usually range from two to nine stones. If the gap between two players is larger than nine stones, you may be better off playing on a smaller board, although as a teaching method sometimes thirteen handicap stones are used on the full-sized board. There is no formal placement for thirteen handicap stones. Putting four extra stones on the 7-7 or on the 3-3 points is a reasonable idea.

In handicap Go, White plays first.

Diagram 2. This is a typical two-stone handicap game. (Even with only one extra stone, Black's advantage here is too large for official competition between professional players these days.) White, the stronger player, plays the first move at 1. Black's first move of the game is at 2, taking a corner. White encloses the corner with 3, and Black takes a side star region at 4.

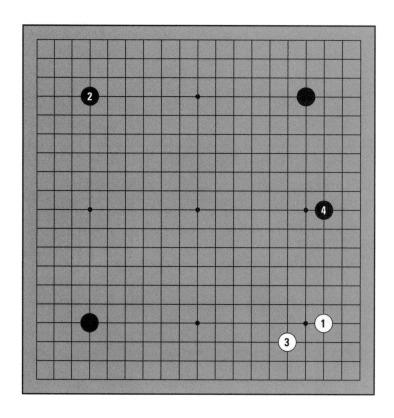

PART THREE

IMPROVEMENT

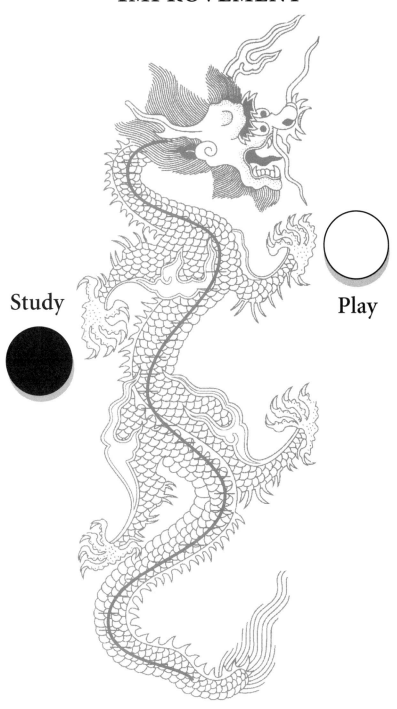

Study

Play

RANKING CHART

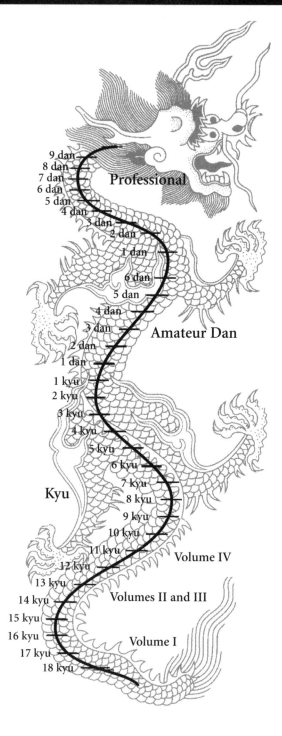

9 dan
8 dan
7 dan
6 dan
5 dan
4 dan
3 dan
2 dan
1 dan

Professional

6 dan
5 dan
4 dan
3 dan
2 dan
1 dan

Amateur Dan

1 kyu
2 kyu
3 kyu
4 kyu
5 kyu
6 kyu
7 kyu
8 kyu
9 kyu
10 kyu
11 kyu
12 kyu
13 kyu
14 kyu
15 kyu
16 kyu
17 kyu
18 kyu

Kyu

Volume IV

Volumes II and III

Volume I

KNOWING THEORY AND TECHNIQUE IS IMPORTANT, BUT IT'S PROBABLY EVEN
MORE IMPORTANT TO BE ABLE TO USE WHAT YOU'VE LEARNED IN REAL
GAMES.

HERE ARE TWENTY-FIVE QUESTIONS COVERING THE MATERIAL IN THIS BOOK.
TRY TO SOLVE EACH PROBLEM BEFORE TURNING THE PAGE. THERE IS A
CHART AT THE END TO ASSESS YOUR SCORE.

1. White has just cut two stones. There are a lot of big points that Black wants to
play. Where is a good place for Black to play now?

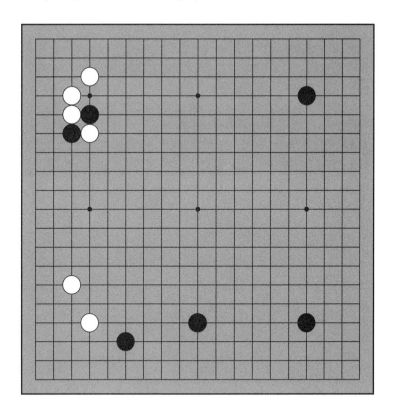

1. Playing on the side star point at 1, building a big framework, is very good.

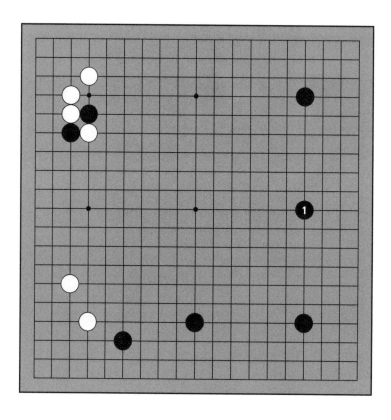

2. When Black connects at 1, White answers at 2. Where does Black play next?

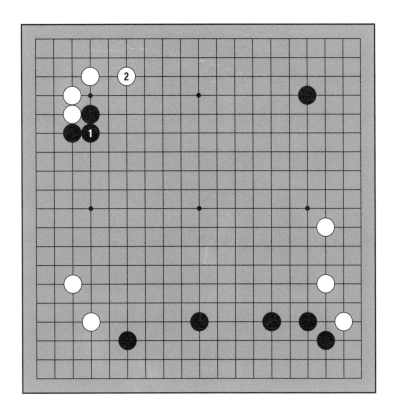

3. Black's area on the lower side is very loose. Where should White invade?

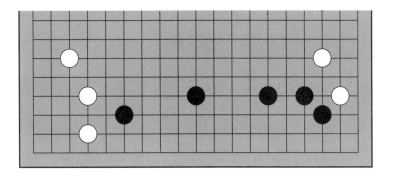

2a. The three-point extension at Black 3 is standard. (Half-credit for other moves in the left side star region.)

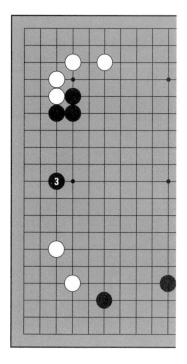

2b. If Black doesn't make a base, White can attack at 4.

3 elsewhere

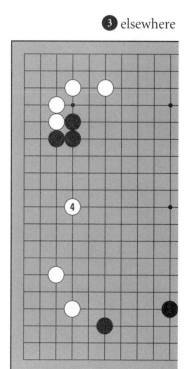

1. White 1 is the invasion point in this position.

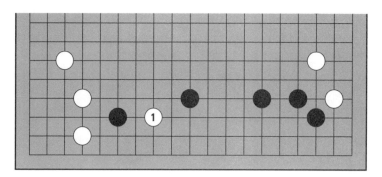

4. How should White play to save the marked stones?

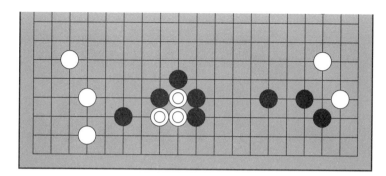

5. White has just caught the marked black stone. How can Black use it as a sacrifice to capture the four marked white stones?

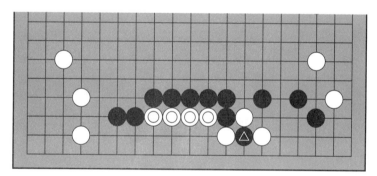

6. When Black comes out at 1, White pushes at 2. Where should Black play next?

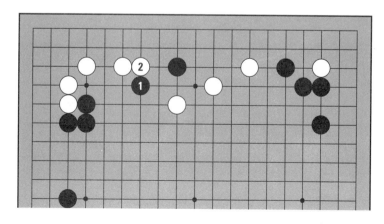

4. White plays atari at 1. When Black connects at 2, White connects at 3. Now White is out and Black's lone stone is in serious difficulty.

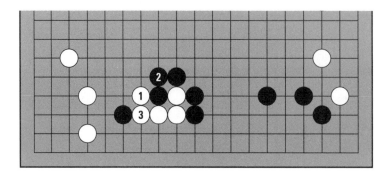

5. After Black plays atari at 1 and White captures at 2, Black can catch White's four stones with 3.

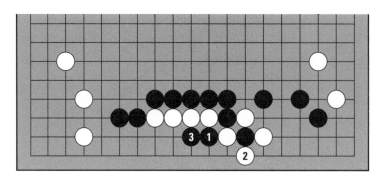

6. Black needs to connect at 3. If Black doesn't answer, White can play there and Black's stone on the upper side is cut off without eyes.

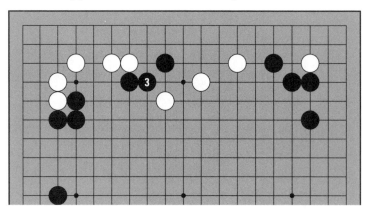

7. When Black plays 1, where does White play? Try to find a move that helps neutralize Black's thickness in the center.

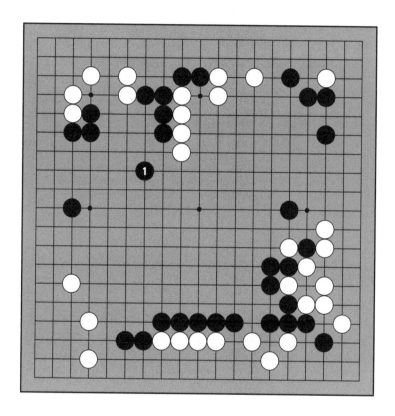

8. White pushes at 1. Where should Black play?

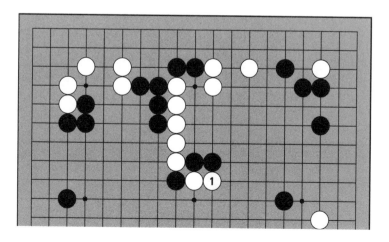

7. The one-point jump at White 2, neutralizing Black's center, is correct. If Black plays at 3, White jumps again at 4. (Half credit for 2 at A.)

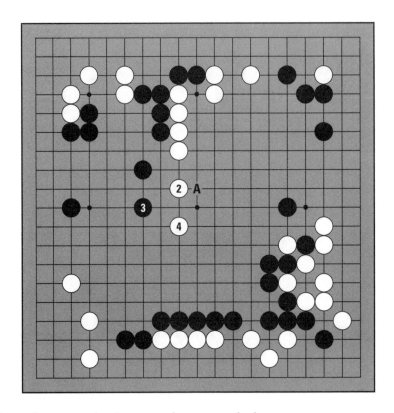

8. Black needs to extend at 2 to save the two marked stones.

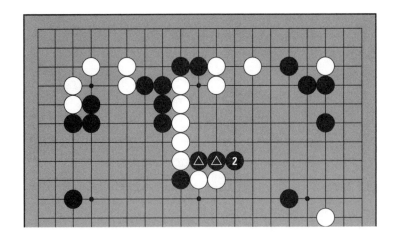

9. White has just captured the black stone that was at A with 1. If Black wants to kill White's marked center group, where should Black play?

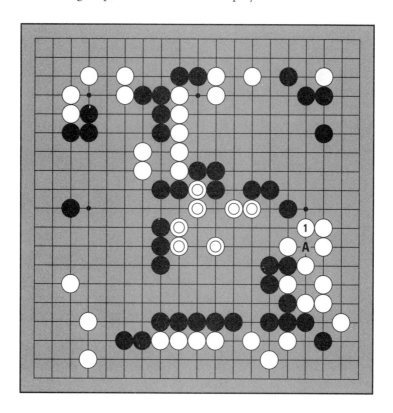

10. Black to play. Try to kill the white group in the corner.

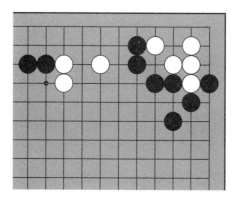

9. Cutting off White's life line at 2 is correct. White doesn't have enough room to live in the center.

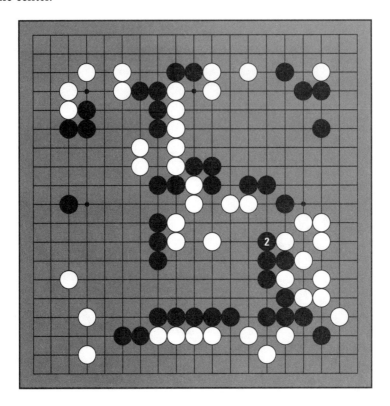

10a. Black 1 is the vital point. (Pushing in at A also works.)

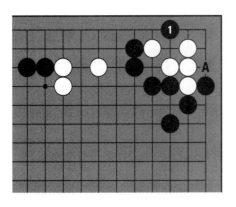

Continuation: If White blocks at 2, Black pushes in at 3 and prevents White from making two eyes at 5. If White captures two stones at A, Black can play the throw-in at Black ●, so White is dead.

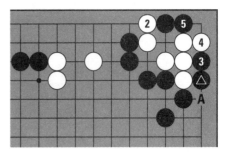

11. White's turn. Try to save White ◎.

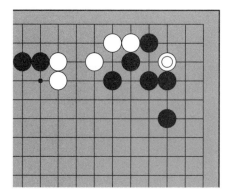

12. White to play. Can you find the big endgame move on the right side?

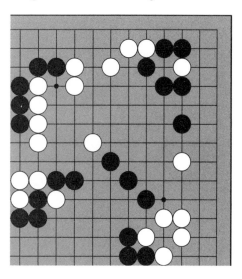

13. In this nine-stone handicap game, White jumps out at 1. What's a good move for Black?

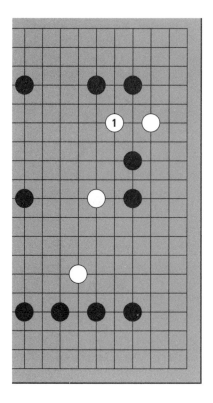

11a. Cutting at 1 doesn't work. Black catches White with 2 and 4.

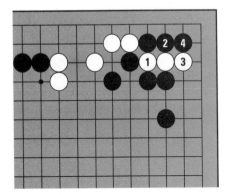

11b. Crossing under with White 1 and 3 is correct.

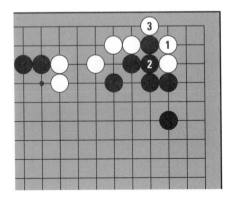

12. The diagonal at White 1 on the edge, expanding White's side area while reducing and threatening Black's corner area, is a big endgame move.

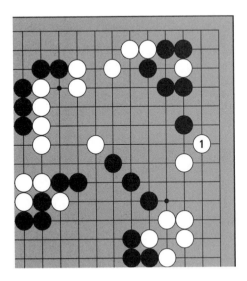

13. Black should move out into the center with 2. Attaching at A instead of Black 2 is also all right.

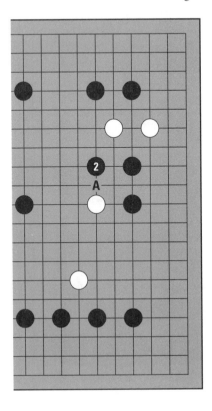

14. When Black plays atari at 1, White runs at 2. Next, if Black wants to come out with the group on the right side where should Black play?

15. Black's ten-stone group and White's seven-stone group on the right side are both cut off, and so far neither has two eyes. How can Black kill White's group?

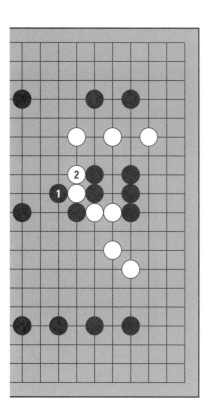

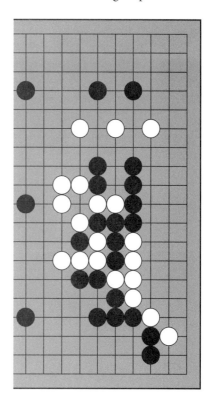

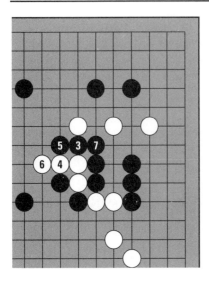

14. Playing atari at Black 3 is correct. White runs at 4, Black pushes at 5 and connects out at 7. (Half-credit for Black 3 at 7.)

15a. Black can reduce White's eye space with 1. If White plays at 4, Black can kill at 5. (If White A, Black crosses under at B.)

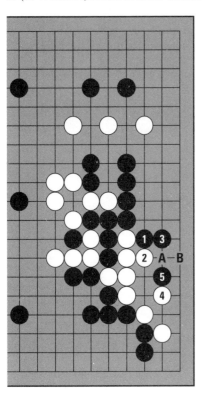

15b. The cut at Black 1 and hane at 3 also work. (If White A, Black B, making the capture of Black 1 a false eye.)

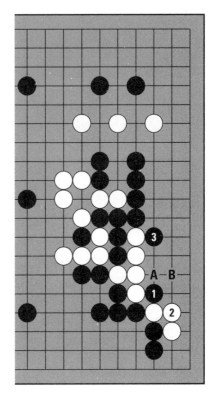

16. White's group on the lower right side looks alive, but it has a big weakness. Can you find a way to kill White?

17. White extends at 1, plotting to capture the big black group on the right side. Where does Black need to play?

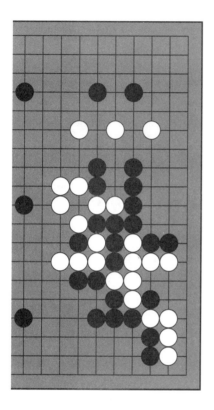

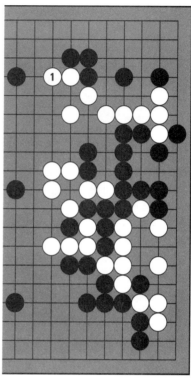

16. Black 1 is the vital point. If White plays atari at 2, Black can set up a snap-back with 3.

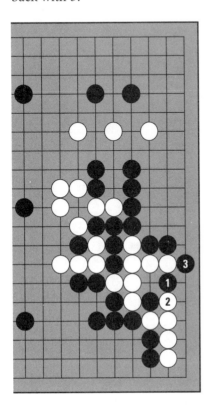

17. Black needs to make two eyes with 2. (Black 2 at A also lives.)

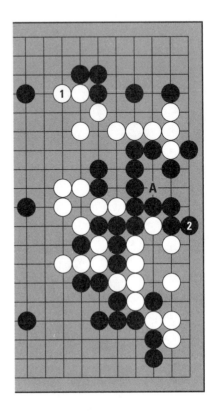

18. White's stones on the lower side aren't completely secure. Where should Black play?

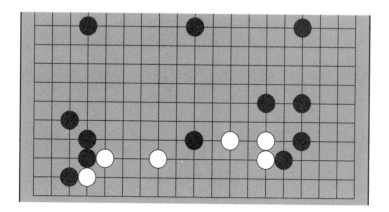

19. In this three-stone handicap game, when Black played 1, White grabbed the lower side star region with 2. Black wants to attack White's stones on the right side. What's a good way to do so?

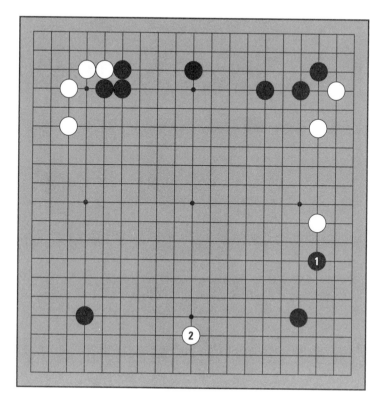

18. Black should separate White's groups with 1. Black 1 at A or B is also okay.

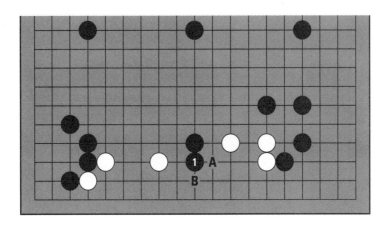

19. Jumping in and fighting with Black 3 is a good move. If White escapes at 4, Black gives chase with 5, putting pressure on White's lone stone on the lower right side as well. Black 3 at A is also correct.

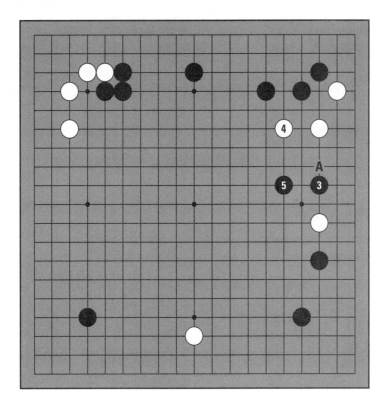

20. Black's turn—can you find a surrounding move that makes it difficult for White's marked stone to escape?

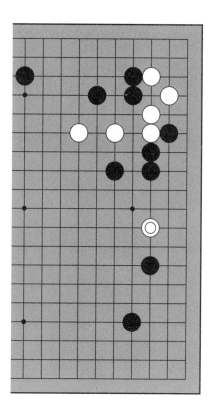

21. When Black blocks at 1, where does White need to play for the group on the upper side to live?

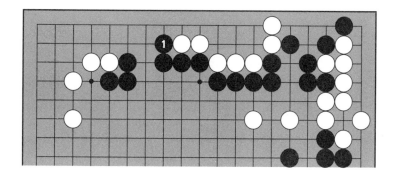

20. Capping with Black 1 is good.

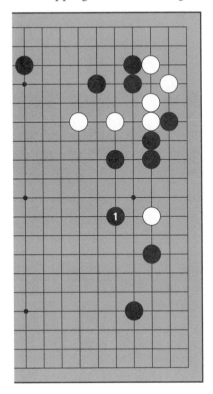

21a. White 2 is the vital point. (2 at A or B would also live.)

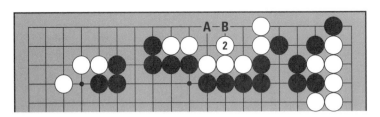

21b. If White plays at 2 here, Black can kill at 3.

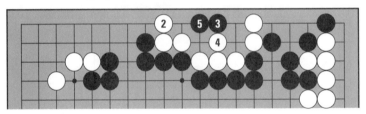

22. White's group on the right side
is in danger. How can it escape?

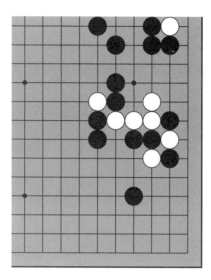

23. White's group on the lower right can be killed.
Where should White play to make two eyes?

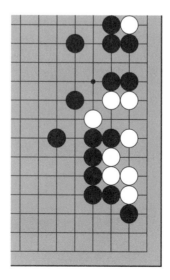

22. Playing atari at 1 is the only way out. Continuing, White pushes again at 3 and turns at 5.

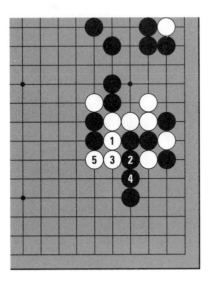

23. If White plays at 1, she lives. White 1 at A also works.

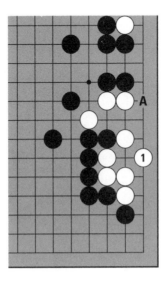

24. How can the white group live?

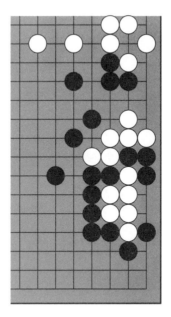

25. Try to protect the territory on the right side while preventing White's group on the lower side from making a secure base.

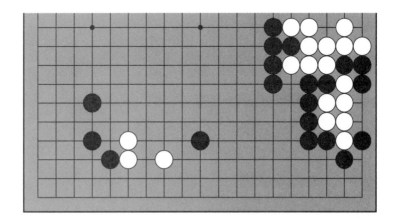

24. White plays at 1. If Black blocks at 2, White makes a second eye at 3.

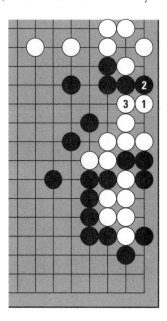

25. The iron pillar at Black 1, protecting Black's area on the right side and putting pressure on White's group, is correct.

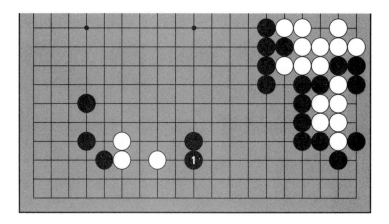

Scoring

Multiply the number of questions you answered correctly by four to determine your score

Above 84: . . . . .Excellent

60-80: . . . . .Good

24-56: . . . . .Average

12-20: . . . . .Needs a little work

below 12: . . . . .Review this book before moving to Volume IV

3-3 point

san-san in Japanese
sam-sam in Korean

3-4 point

komoku in Japanese
somok in Korean

approach

generic term for
opening hostilities
against a stone in a
corner

**approach
knight's**

(usually third-line)
play that has a
knight's move rela-
tionship with a
(usually 3-4 or star
point) opposing
stone

**approach
one-point**

(usually fourth-line)
play that has a one-
point relationship
with a (usually 3-4
or star point)
opposing stone

atari

move that reduces
liberties to one, i.e.,
threatens to capture

**atari
double**

move that threatens
to capture two
stones or groups
simultaneously

attachment

an initial contact
play on an opposing
stone

base see **eye space**

bent three see **eye
shape**

block

a play "in front of"
opposing stones,
preventing them
from continuing
along a line

cap

a stone with a one-
point jump relation-
ship to a stone clos-
er to the edge

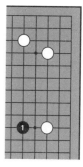

capture

removal of stone(s)
when all their liber-
ties are blocked

clamp
attaching on two
opposing liberties of
a stone of the other
color

compensation
points given to
counteract one side's
advantage
komi in Japanese
dom in Korean

connection
generic term for a
link between stones
that prevents them
from being cut

**connection
solid**
stones that cannot
be cut because they
are connected by
lines

**connection
knight's**
indirect connection,
stones can't be cut
because a cutting
stone could be cap-
tured in a ladder

**connection
tiger's mouth**
indirect connection,
stones can't be cut
because a cutting
stone could be cap-
tured immediately

counting estimat-
ing the score during
the game

cross under
connection on the
edge under oppos-
ing stones

crosscut
each side is cut in
two by the other

cut
generic term for pre-
venting the connec-
tion of opposing
stones

cutting point
point where a group
can be cut

dan master rank,
see chart page 123

death
the condition of
being capturable,
surrounded without
two eyes

descend
extending down to
the edge

diagonal
indirect connection—a move placed diagonally next to another one of your stones

dual life
position where both sides are cut by each other and neither has two eyes, but neither side can be captured

enclosure
generic term for surrounding corner territory

enclosure knight's
stones of the same color on the 3-4 and the 5-3 points (also, on the star and 6-3 points)

enclosure one-point
stones of the same color on the 3-4 and the 5-4 points (also, on the star and 6-4 points)

extend
move on a liberty adjacent to another one of your stones

extension
generic term for a move on the side to make a base or territory

extension three-point
extension three points away from your other stone(s)

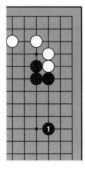

extension two-point
extension two points away from your other stone(s)

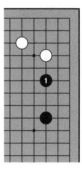

eye
point of territory, in the context of life and death

eye false
point surrounded by stones of the same color not all connected to each other

eye shape
specific configuration of an area for making eyes

eye shape bent three
type of eye space with three adjacent points of territory in a triangle

eye space
also **base**
area for making eyes

fourth line
also *power line*
the fourth line from the edge of the board

framework
large potential territory area not yet impervious to enemy invasion or reduction

gup see kyu

hane
also *turn the corner*
a blocking "quick turn" leaving a cut at A, playing on two adjacent liberties of an opposing stone.

hane
double
a hane in response to a hane in response to a hane

heavy
unwieldy, inflexible, overconcentrated stones (conpare with *thickness*)

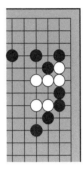

high
stone or position on the fourth line or higher, closer to the center star point

influence
also **power**
attribute of stones on the fourth line or higher facing relatively unplayed areas

invasion
also *jump in*
move inside opponent's area to prevent it from becoming territory

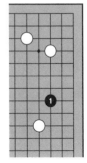

iron pillar
from a stone on the fourth line on the side, descending, usually to prevent a slide

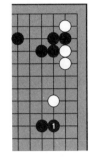

jump
generic term for a one- or two-point jump

jump
   one-point
move one point along a line away from your stone(s)

jump
   two-point
move two points along a line away from your stone(s)

kill
move that surrounds stones that don't have two eyes, or prevents surrounded stones from making two eyes

knight's move
play one point along a line and then a diagonal away from another one of your stones

ko
a position where a stone that has just captured is itself in atari, that could repeat endlessly without the rule that one may not immediately capture a stone that has just captured in ko

ko threat
interposing move that prevents endless repetition in ko (after playing the threat at 2, if White answers, Black can capture with 4).

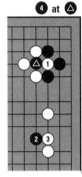

kyu a lower rank, see chart page 128

ladder
capturing technique involving keeping stone(s) in atari and driving them to the edge

ladder breaker
an opposing stone along a ladder's path, that prevents a capture by the ladder

large knight's move
play two points along a line and then a diagonal away from another one of your stones

liberty
line emerging from a
stone

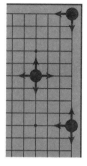

life
condition of being
impervious to capture,
having two eyes

low
stone or position on
the third line or lower,
closer to the edge

neutral point
point where neither
side can make territory
dame in Japanese
gongbae in Korean

peep
threat to cut by pre-
venting a tiger's mouth

pin
a capturing technique
which takes advantage
of multiple weak points

pincer
play usually one,
two, or three points
away on the third or
fourth line from an
approach stone

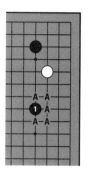

**positional judg-
ment** see **counting**

potential
point(s) in an area
that if stone(s) of an
opposing color are
placed there may
prevent it from
becoming territory

power
also **influence**
attribute of stones
facing relatively
unplayed areas on
the fourth line or
higher

pull back
after an attachment,
extending "back-
wards" to link the
attaching stone to
another one of your
stones

push
extending to a point
adjacent to a stone
of the opposing
color

read
visualize or anticipate an ensuing sequence of moves

second line
second line from the edge of the board

sente
also *initiative*
1. playing first
2. a move that should be answered

sente endgame
endgame move that should be answered

sente reverse
move that is not or does not retain sente, but prevents a sente play by the opponent

shoulder hit
move on the fourth line with a diagonal relationship to an opposing stone on the third line

side star region
region around a side star point

sleeper
stone strategically placed for possible activation later (also called *aji* in Japanese)

slide
play under opponent's stone(s), usually on the second line and having a knight's move relationship to another one of your stones

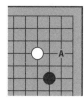

snapback
one-move capturing technique involving a throw-in, utilizing opponent's shortage of liberties

spike
pushing completely through opposing stones

standard sequence
established patterns, usually in the corners, that are reasonable for both sides
joseki in Japanese
jeongsuk in Korean

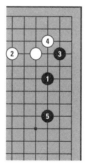

star point
one of nine darker points on the board

territory
points that are or will be surrounded by walls of one color

thickness*
outward facing, connected groups of stones

third line
also *territory line*
third line from the edge of the board

throw-in
bait or sacrifice used to reduce opponent's liberties or eye space

tiger's mouth
three stones in a "V" shape

turtle back
resulting six-stone formation after capturing two stones

weak point see **cutting point**

wedge
single stone (not connected by lines to other stones) played in between the opponent's one-point jump

vital point
key point for life and death, often the center of symmetry

vulgar
move you play that
1. makes territory,
2. increases thickness,
or 3. stabilizes groups for your opponent

*It's sometimes hard to distinguish between thick stones and heavy ones. Basically, thickness is good, and heaviness is too much of a good thing – a heavy or over-concentrated group is inefficient becasue the same results could have been had using fewer stones.

INDEX

Note on names: Chinese, Japanese, and Korean names in this book are given family name first.

The American Go Association

Since 1926, the national organization to promote the game of go

Full membership for one year is just $25 and includes:

• AGA starter packet

• Subscription to the *American Go Journal*
  a quarterly magazine featuring amateur and professional games from around the world
  special articles for beginners, and other fun stuff

• The *American Go Newsletter*
  providing the latest news on club activities
  a calendar of upcoming events, and tournament results

• Eligibility to compete in local and regional AGA tournaments
  including US Go Congress events and the US Open

• Official rating in the AGA's computerized national rating system

• Information and support
  to help you form your own club or educational program
  or find players in your area

For more information or to join, write to:
AGA—Dept. G, PO Box 397, Old Chelsea Station, New York, NY 10113-0397

Learn to Play Go
Volume IV: Battle Strategies

Janice Kim 1 dan
Jeong Soo-hyun 8 dan

Volume V

coming
1998

Volume VI

Volume VII

Volume VIII

Volume IX

About the Authors

Janice Kim was born in Illinois in 1969. She entered the professional dan ranks in Korea in 1987, the only Westerner ever to do so. She won the Fuji Women's Championship in 1984, took second place in the World Youth Championship in 1985, and third place in the EBS Cup in 1994.

A graduate of New York University, Ms. Kim lives in Manhattan. She teaches at go workshops and a summer go camp and has regular columns in the *American Go Journal* and *Baduk Monthly*. In 1997 Ms. Kim founded Samarkand, a mail-order company that carries go books and equipment.

Timothy Greenfield-Sanders

Jeong Soo-hyun was born in Korea in 1956. Since entering the professional dan ranks in 1973, he has played in numerous championship leagues, winning the Shin Wang title in 1986. He was promoted to 8 dan in 1994, and 9 dan in 1997.

A well-known teacher, Mr. Jeong has written more than twenty books and is a popular commentator on Korean television. He served a term as President of the Korean Professional Go Association, the youngest person ever to hold this prestigious post. Now a university professor teaching go, he lives in Seoul with his wife and two children.

Hankook Kiwon